CROSSING THE LINE IN 250 CHARACTERS OR LESS

(Posts on Politics, Prurience, Protestantism, Patriotism and Preposterousness)

(Dana Nuheritage)

This work is dedicated to my mother, Mary Kathryn. She prepared me for my departure from her into life and her departure from me into the next life. She used to say, "Boy, if you can successfully manage your home, you can successfully manage any business. But if you can't manage yourself, you won't be able to manage anything else." And one of the greatest admonitions she gave me was, "Boy, don't be afraid to go out into the deep water." Because, as I now know, whether we swim in three feet of water or a bottomless ocean, our strokes don't change.

Table of Contents

Preface

This is the first book of a trilogy. In this initial installment we meet Dana Nuheritage and one of his infinite alter egos, Radu the Beneficial Blogger. Nuheritage has much wisdom and insight borne of his life experiences and ancestral knowledge. From his earliest days he recalls his mother telling him of the sayings his maternal great-grandmother told his maternal grandmother who in turn told his mother. These sayings were imbued with knowledge and wisdom extant for millennia before his great-grandmother's time. But more important than hearing the sayings, because we all have, Nuheritage implemented them in his life. The many times that he failed to heed 'the moral of the story' reinforced the truth of the sayings.

This "blog-alogue" (blog + dialogue) begins on September 11, 2009 and ends two years later during the 10 year anniversary of the 9-11 attacks. Ten years earlier, Nuheritage, an attorney by trade, had a very challenging 2001. His home was foreclosed on and he filed bankruptcy. Also that year his license to practice law was suspended for 5 years. This suspension, like his 2010 DUI arrest blogged about at length in Chapters 1 and 2, was motivated by factors well beyond the truthfulness of the allegations that gave rise to it. Also in 2001, he went through a very ugly divorce categorized by scandalously false charges of spousal abuse leveled against him. Ultimately, indisputable evidence proved that the charges were outrageous lies. Nevertheless, the time between the persistent filing of these false charges and Nuheritage's vindication added to the many challenges of 2001.

But he survived that year helped by the ancestral teachings passed on by his mother. Through blogging on social media, he passes the teachings on to a public in desperate need of them. His method is to combine insight with laughter.

Below you will read commentary and reflections from Nuheritage posted on 'MyFace'. The posts are reproduced as then written with limited to no revision. To the extent any posts were edited, it was done for the purpose of clarification. Some reproductions include selected portions of or the entire thread responses to Nuheritage's original post. MyFace limits the initial post of a thread to 250 characters or less. There is no limit placed on subsequent responses on a thread.

Introduction

In this blog-alogue you will read selected thoughts and opinions of Dana Nuheritage, the Beneficial Blogger, posted on the social network <u>MY-FACEtiousness.com</u>. They are at times poignant, provocative, comedic, mischievous and offensive. Dana Nuheritage is but one of an infinite number of aliases of our subject blogger. He has many more than I can follow or recollect to you. You, mercifully so, will only follow the postings of two, Nuheritage and Radu. However, he makes passing references to some of his infinite alter-egos.

The public generally refers to <u>MY-FACEtiousness.com</u> as MyFace or MF. There are almost as many opinions about MF as there are users. Nuheritage calls it a monument to vanity, self-absorption and narcissim, amongst other things. Many subscribers live their lives on MyFace before the public. Some find it intrusive while others find logging in on a regular basis a necessity of life in the 21st century. Nuheritage believes that MF is whatever you make it.

Female subscribers are known as 'she-shushes' and the males are 'he-shushes'. To follow postings on MyFace, if not already, you should familiarize yourself with the various expedited writing styles utilized by many who regularly visit the site. The styles are a blend of techno jargon, hip-hop phoneticism, grunge expediting spellings and teen texting conventions. At first glance, the script utilized by Nuheritage may appear distracting and confusing. However, because of the repetitive nature of the language used, one will gain immediate fluency after a page or two.

Humans become fluent speakers and readers of any language by immersing themselves in that language. Your immersion into the language of MF and Nuheritage begins with a thread from a messageboard Nuheritage regularly posts to. The members of this messageboard are aficionados of club salsa. The excerpted thread will acclimate the uninitiated reader to much of the phonetic spelling presented in this blog-alogue.

Chronic texters and users of instant messaging services on computers and smart phones will not take immediate note of the deviations in standard, American spellings. They are already accustomed to it.

The following thread appears on a messageboard devoted to salsa dancing, club style -- not ballroom. Nuheritage posts under the alias Bailandus. Three other principle posters are Salsa Soldier, Guajiro and John. Salsa Soldier is a Puerto Rican Research Scientist. Guajiro is an engineer of Cuban decent and graduate of the University of Michigan. John is a computer programmer. At the time of these postings, the messageboard had recently instituted a rule that required all those who posted in Spanish, which many did, to provide an English translation to their posts. The Spanish translations provided below are those of the author.

Posted Sep 6, 2007 12:28 PM: Liz

Should people offer advice or critique other dancers while they are dancing????????.

Posted Sep 6, 2007 12:36 PM: Bailandus

The 2 of the wisest things my grandfthr ever tld me were:

1) "The bst wy 2 loose ur money is 2 lt ppl knw u have it"; &

2) "Dnt gv advc unlss u r askd 4 it." Stated dffrntly, "Speak not in the ears of a fool for he will despise ur wsdm."

Posted Sep 6, 2007 1:15 PM: Liz

ur grndmthr is 1 smrt wmn!

Posted Sep 6, 2007 1:20 PM: Guajiro

D q cñ stn hblnd stds... ?

[De que coño estan hablando ustedes? (What the fuck are you two talking about?)]

Posted Sep 6, 2007 1:28 PM: Salsa Soldier

Crjo, qe tnto dsprte hbln ustds! Nssto un trgo pa embrchrme!

[Carajo que tanto disparate hablan ustedes. Necesito un trago para emboracharme! (Hell, you all are talking much nonsense! I need a drink to get drunk)]

Posted Sep 6, 2007 1:32 PM: Guajiro

j j j j j j j j [ha ha ha ha.....]

stn cnfndndm cñ! Nssto un trgo tmbn!

[estan confundiendome coño! Necesito un trago tambien

(you are all confusing me damn it! I need a drink too)]

Posted Sep 6, 2007 1:35 PM: Salsa Soldier

Un lngje scrto pa cnfndns! Crvza, qro crvza!

[Un lenguaje secreto para confundirnos! Cerveza, quiero cerveza! (A secret language to confuse us! Beer, I want beer!)]

Posted Sep 6, 2007 1:37 PM: Guajiro

h h h h j j j j [ha ha ha ha ......]

qro crvza y qro mntrt! Rn y Cccl! j j j j j

[Quiero cerveza and mentirita! Ron y coca cola! je je je je je (I want a beer and a rum and coke! ha ha ha ha)] -- *Many Latinos refer to a rum and coke as a Cuba libre (a free Cuba). Some Cubans refer to it as a Mentirita (a little lie), i.e. Cuba is not free.*

Posted Sep 6, 2007 1:37 PM: Salsa Soldier

R we sppsed to trnslat ths?

Posted Sep 6, 2007 1:38 PM: Sheila

Ys

Posted Sep 6, 2007 1:38 PM: Guajiro

w'r n trbl!

Posted Sep 6, 2007 1:42 PM: Casandra

You guys have me laughing so hard at my desk that tears are rolling down my face!!!

OOOOps sorry....I included the vowels!!

Posted Sep 6, 2007 1:44 PM: Salsa Soldier

U wll b xcmmncatd!

Posted Sep 6, 2007 1:47 PM: Salsa Soldier

Blam it all on Blnds! He strtd it.

Posted Sep 6, 2007 2:05 PM: Cathy

You guys are killing me!!!! You would think I was undergoing an eye exam!

Posted Sep 6, 2007 2:07 PM: Sheila

I'm trying to figure out how to throw pig latin into the mix...

Posted Sep 6, 2007 2:10 PM: Bailandus

 'ur grndmthr is 1 smrt wmn'!

@ Liz: Btu ym grnadftahre si mael.

U knw lteter odrer si nto taht improtnat, fi ouy dnot laraeyd nkow htat. Dna vwoles rea a mdoner dya invnetoin.

Posted Sep 6, 2007 2:12 PM: Salsa Soldier

Wow. U thrw ths nto a whl nw lvl! Now cthy wll rlly b squntng. Bt I did undrstnd all of it.

Posted Sep 6, 2007 2:18 PM: Bailandus

Hte mnid sees waht ti wants 2 c. Tahts ywh flkos cna dnace fof
baet nda sitll eb hppay.
S bn profndo.

[Es bien profundo (It's very deep)]

Posted Sep 6, 2007 2:20 PM: Salsa Soldier

KO, I yllear eend ot teg kcab ot orkw os tops akingm em ghaul.

Posted Sep 6, 2007 2:23 PM: Guajiro

peolpe wlli raed thsi adn sya WFT?!

Posted Sep 6, 2007 2:30 PM: Bailandus

Does WTF mean, wow that's funny?

Posted Sep 6, 2007 2:33 PM: Guajiro

or Wednesday, Thursday, Friday

Posted Sep 6, 2007 2:43 PM: Nenis

omg u gys r 2 fnny ... my stmch hrts frm lghng so mch ...lol

Posted Sep 6, 2007 3:49 PM: Alvin

orijauwg dna slaas loedsir era draobegassem srekcajih.

When will it end?

Posted Sep 6, 2007 4:34 PM: John

I THINK I WILL JUST START TYPING IN CAPS ALL THE
TIME. I KNOW PEOPLE JUST LOVE THAT!

Posted Sep 6, 2007 4:36 PM: Guajiro

John.... y0u c@n wr!+3 !n c0mpu+er l@ngu@g3.

Posted Sep 6, 2007 5:14 PM: John

True. Here I go for the real techies on the message board:

Procedure communicate(annoy, becute, isfun);

```
sentencelast: = "Isn't this great!";
sentencemiddle: = "I can write sentences in code";
sentencelast: = "I bet people will love this!";
close procedure
Open procedure begin
print (x32 y344, sentencefirst + " " sentencemiddle + " " +
sentencelast)
close procedure.
```

That's the easy stuff. If you like, I can just do binary code!

Posted Sep 6, 2007 5:17 PM: Guajiro

John... There's only 1 or 0 kind of people in this world, those who understand binary and those that do not.

Posted Sep 6, 2007 5:39 PM: John

True dat. Do you have a secret decoder ring? In binary computer code, this is what happened when a woman wrongflly accused me of staring at her chest while dancing:

```
01000010 01100101 00100000 01110011 01110101
01110010 01100101 00100000 01110100 01101111
00100000 01100100 01110010 01101001 01101110
01101011 00100000 01111001 01101111 01110101
01110010 00100000 01101111 01110110 01100001
01101100 01110100 01101001 01101110 01100101
```

Posted Sep 6, 2007 5:43 PM: Guajiro

011001110110101111011011110110010000100000011011110110111001100101001000000110101001101111011010000110
1110

Posted Sep 6, 2007 5:47 PM: Bailandus

Stop it! U 2 r killing me. I hvn't hrd tht one, or zero, n a lng time.

Posted Sep 6, 2007 6:07 PM: John

01010100 01101000 01100001 01101110 01101011 00100000 01111001 01101111 01110101!!!

Posted Sep 6, 2007 6:19 PM: Bailandus

Calm dwn R2D2. U were rt 2 defend urslf. She desrvd it. It was just a dance. Does anyone else agree w/ John?

Posted Sep 7, 2007 9:08 AM: Mein

'Lteter odrer si nto taht improtnat, fi ouy dnot laraeyd nkow htat. Dna vwoles rea a mdoner dya invnetoin.'

Yes, you can jumble all the letters within a word. The "rule" is if you keep the first and the last letters intact, it would make reading almost like normal and you won't have to pause to figure a word out, if you didn't.

Try to read this as fast as you can:

Tihs is rlleay fnuny and to tnhik taht wirtnig in spnasih-olny had cuaesd smoe ppleoe hadeahces bfreoe. I wndoer waht jlemubd ltteres in sapnish wluod do to tehm. But tehn, the wrsoe is gteting rid of vlewos form snsipah wrdos. Taht rlelay teaxs the mnid. ugh. Taht, or I wluod jsut need to let it go. The Ckeczs, Saolvks, the Hngauinars and the Ploes had it rhgit wtih teihr all cnanosont wdros. Sramt.

Posted Sep 7, 2007 10:42 AM: Liz

I'm glad you LOCOS are back to writing "normal." That other stuff was giving me a headache.

Posted Sep 7, 2007 2:47 PM: Salsa Soldier

With the exception of 3 words that held me up a little "jumbled, "taxes" and "Smart", I read this as fast as I would read anything else. Cool.

Posted Sep 8, 2007 8:49 AM: Mein

Cool huh? :-)

Yes, primarily, the idea is that when you read (normally, that is) you don't really look at each letter in each word; nor look at each word in every line. That's how you can read fast - you just kinda skim through. The eye looks at whole sections of the line and may skip words entirely because they're within that field of the eye's focus at the moment. It's more like a smooth, flat stone being thrown across a quiet pond, hitting the surface of the water only a few times; rather than a little balloon icon jumping about or what have you in a Karaoke sing-along captions on a tv monitor.

But also, longer words may present more trouble, like "jumbled"-- it's not so commonly used and it's, well, a longer word. The eye would have had to settle on a longer word as a point of focus and then one would really have to know what the word is if it's jumbled (Scrabble experience would help). Additionally, the context of the sentence plays in as well, hence, "texas" won't really fit in (cuz it's BIG, haha).

Facility in the language would definitely help. So, if it were in Sapnsih, I'd have real trouble.

I wouldn't recommend, however, writing in "jumble-ese" because one's spelling abilities might suffer (or maybe it won't --- might improve your Scrabble skills, though).

--END THREAD --

After completing that thread your knowledge of internet age spelling and prose is abundantly sufficient to easily read this blog-alogue. The grammar is now present but you may need to increase your vocabulary to understand the meaning of many acronyms used through the ether. The acronyms used within these pages will be clearly understood by any reader through context clues alone.

CHAPTER ONE

Fall 2009

Bombs Fall on Those Who Drop Bombs

Dana Nuheritage

The lesson of 9/11 for me is: Bombs fall on those that drop bombs. So lets remember those who died in NYC, the Pentagon & PA. Ass well, let's remember those who were killed n Vietnam, Cambodia, Laos, Hiroshima, Nagasaki, Dresden, Libya, Baghdad, Afghanistan and else where from ordnance dropped by u know who.
September 11, 2009 at 10:31am

This summer a 27 year old new father & husband on my soccer team died on his motorcycle and a colleague survived an aortic dissection. In response, I've decided to post some of my musings on MF and change my

name to Ecclestheasticus. Maybe some/more good will come out of this shrine to vanity, self-absorption and indulgency.
October 8, 2009 at 3:30am

Ppl say thy dont do Hllwn b/c it's based on a pagan holiday. N tht case, u shldn't celebrate Xmas during the winter solstice. Every holiday is based on a pagan holiday, maybe xcpt for national independence day celebrations. Since the invention of agriculture humans hv made observances of at least 4 times n the year: when crops r planted & harvested and when the sun is at its highest & lowest in the sky, summer/winter solstice. If u celebrate any holiday during those times, ur celebration is based on a pagan holiday. So let a kid get some candy and women dress like hookers.
October 29, 2009 at 10:40am W/o any prompting from me, my 11yr old son admitted that his recent poor grades in math are a result of him not paying attention n class and not studying enough. All my talking is not in vain. "Heaven or Hell is the life we live made for us by our own decisions."
November 5, 2009 at 1:42pm

Does god have a penis? If ppl refer to god ass "he", does that mean god is a man, i.e. not a woman? And if he is a man, doesn't that mean he has a penis [B/c genitalia is what distinguishes men from women. Right?]? And if he is a man w/ a penis, w/ whom does he copulate? I have read that "god is a spirit" like the wind. Does the wind have genitalia?
December 19, 2009 at 5:41am

The misuse of the word "love" saddens me more than the observance of Xmas n this country. Some r heard 2 say: thy love chicken; thy love their car; thy love sports or thy fell n love. If 1 can fall n love, 1 can easily fall out of it. But if love is built, it has a greater chance of enduring. So don't love anything tht doesn't hv the ability 2 love u back.
December 19, 2009 at 5:49am

A friend asked me what was my dream car. I responded, "I don't dream of cars." Someone starving will dream of food. The homeless dream of a

roof over their head. The lost person headed nowhere dreams of a car to take him there.
December 31, 2009 at 7:27am

If u can see or touch a thing it will ultimately cease to exist. Who u really r is the thing u can't see. The important things n life r this way, eg. air, love, sacrifice. U can't see them or touch them. Likewise, when u realize who u r, what person will b able to touch u?
December 31, 2009 at 7:35am

Don't try to gain friends. Do what u know to be right. By doing so, some u'll offend and some u'll win.
December 31, 2009 at 7:38am

Posted after televangelist Pat Robinson attributed the January 12, 2010 magnitude 7.0 earthquake that struck Haiti to that nation making a pact with the devil to end French colonial rule and slavery.

Y do so mny tune daily 2 hear the ramblngs of a man whose ignrnce of the Bible is only surpssd by his lack of knwldg of wrld hstry? R we 2 blv tht god wld nvr act 2 end genocide, slavery, mass rape & torture? No, 2 secure relief frm tht, u must cnsort w/ the devil. A cursory reading of history shws tht the genesis of Haiti's prblm was the collaboration of imperialists nations 2 mk it a lessn 4 othr slaves thru out the Americas, just like Cuba 2day.
January 14, 2010 at 11:48am

Saw a woman driving on an obvious, driver-side, front, flat ystrdy. Pointed it out 2 her. Still n her car she said, "The car did feel a lil fnny." She got out the car; looked at the tire and said, "No wonder I didn't notice that. The top of the tire isn't flat like the bottom is."
January 16, 2010 at 11:13am

CMTSU! Thursday a friend revealed to me her suspicions about the Haiti earthquake. She thght it was a conspiracy by developed countries. "After all", she said, "since the quake registered so high on the Richter Scale, y didn't those countries have time to warn Haiti?" Can't make this stuff up!

January 17, 2010 at 9:23am

Posted after one of the many record snowfalls that blanketed the East Coast during the winter of 2010.

U folk n duh Northeast, enuf w/ duh snow pics alrdy u keep posting. Geeez! We've seen 1000s of them. We get it: If ur house is located outside, it's covered n snow. And ur 60k car is snow packed n front of ur 100k house. U need a garage. Post some pics of duh svelte, bikini girl from ur trip to Bora Bora. & make sure ur gut or thumb is not n duh shot.
February 10, 2010 at 9:37am

Whts the difference btwn a youngin' walking down duh street n thick-soled Timbs wearing baggy jeans that he has to pull up over his draws every 5 mins and a honey @ duh club n a pair of 3", Cum-F-Me pumps wearing a form fitting, black, spandex, micro mini that she has to pull down over her draws every 5 steps? "Looking like a fool w/ ur pants on duh ground. Looking like a fool w/ ur skirt n duh air."
February 14, 2010 at 6:53am

> **Gene** I dont think the honey wears anything under tha mini
> February 14, 2010 at 7:11am

> **Maria** What's with the word 'duh'??
> February 14, 2010 at 7:20am

> **Dana Nuheritage** Maria dats duh neo-urban, hip-hop phonetic, post-sexting, expedited spelling convention dat u wld't understand.
> February 14, 2010 at 11:00am

> **Angela** both look like fools to me.....do they own a mirror? Well give them the benefit of the doubt..... they're standin still in front of the mirror so nothin's dropppin or ridin lol either way guys will still try to

hit that skirt
February 14, 2010 at 12:55pm

Posted after seeing a photo of J.J. from 'Good Times' and controversial, conservative pundit Ann Coulter posing on the red carpet for paparazzi after evidently arriving together for some event.

If Jimmy "J.J." Walker is boinking Ann "duh Maven of duh Radical Right" Coulter, there's somebody 4 u. Butt u might hv 2 date duh person u hate duh most. Hppy V-day all.
February 14, 2010 at 11:06am

Posted during the 2010 Winter Olympics in Vancouver, Canada.

Duh Olympics is duh biggest propaganda tool snc duh 3rd Reich. How often do we hv 2 know duh medal count? R we 2 blv a country's gr8nss is measured by how many medals it wins? Shldnt a ppl b measured by how thy treat: the politically disaffctd, other nations, the environment, recent arrivals and all citizens? America isn't gr8 b/c a chap paid to swim snc youth wins a glorified, rappers' medallion.
February 19, 2010 at 10:30am

> **Jessica** You gotta watch the movie, "Invictus" and you will then appreciate the spirit of the games. I'm not a winter Olympics enthusiast, but I do like that the spirit of healthy competition bringing people from different countries together.
> February 19, 2010 at 1:20pm

> **Dana Nuheritage** Dat's xctly duh point. It's not abt duh spirit of amateur competition. It's abt rich countries 1-upping one another, eg. who can hv duh most elaborate opening ceremony.
> February 19, 2010 at 1:36pm

Gabe Don't get me wrong, I love the Olympics and what it's supposed to stand for. World unity, peaceful competition. But, I remember an Olympics long ago, and they showed the gym where the Russian (I think) gymnasts were training. Anyone of us in the U.S. could join a snazzier gym than what they showed these athletes training in. In America, we do have access to the best training.
February 21, 2010 at 12:49am

Dana Nuheritage America has the best training facilities @ the xpns of wht? I c footage of these mltimillion $ facilities w/ 5 coaches wrkng w/ 1 athlete. Thn I c public school class rooms w/ 40 students per teacher & 1 books.
February 21, 2010 at 9:57am

A good friend tld me he was buying a new home aftr rcntly buying a 5 bdrm "McMansion" tht, w/ only his wife & kid, he had bn living n for lss than 2 years. Responding 2 my nevitabl question, y was he moving, he xplnd dat he & his wife made moe $ last year. Does making moe translate n 2 consuming moe & assuming moe debt? Consumerism, conspicuous consumption & MTV Cribs will make a Redd Foxx, Isaac Hayes, Burt Reynolds, Ed McMahon or MC Hammer out of duh whole nation. Welcome 2 America: "Home of duh greed and financially nslaved."
February 28, 2010 at 11:23am

Jessica Over indulgence, over abundance, mo money = mo' headaches---just to try to maintain it all.
February 28, 2010 at 12:35pm

Penny Moe stuff doesn't equal contentment! With moe stuff r we a blessing to others?
February 28, 2010 at 12:52pm

Zell Big tax break I guess lol. And the down economy is the time to rack up if u have the funds and scores.

Lol
February 28, 2010 at 4:54pm

Dana Nuheritage If dat was duh thinking, Zelly
Zell, u r right. No matter the economic ncntv, do u nd
10 cars and a 7 bdrm house 4 3 ppl. American fami-
lies r gttng smller and our homes r gttng larger. Btwn
McMansions, txtng & iPods, prtty soon kids wont even
hv 2 meet their parents.
March 1, 2010 at 7:09am

For the nxt 18 months I shall be referred to only as Radu Udar Duar
(last name pronounced DWAH). During said period I will not answer
to Dana, Mackimous, Buck, Africanus, Mojtabah, Sadu, Pete, Doo Doo
or Mandingaling. All future requests for interviews from media will b
declined if the proper appellation is not utilized. Dates for my Spring
stand-up tour and tent revival will b forth coming. Look for me on a dais
near u.
March 3, 2010 at 11:20am

Laine Malik But why?
March 3, 2010 at 3:25pm

Dana Nuheritage Y do dogs consume their own fe-
ces?
March 3, 2010 at 3:52pm

Penny Dah?? Auhh! Okay..
March 3, 2010 at 8:42pm

Dana Nuheritage Exactly. My point precisely.
March 4, 2010 at 9:10am

Christen hmmm....this is interesting uncle...Radu
March 4, 2010 at 3:11pm

Finally saw Avatar. Wht is so gr8 abt tht movie? Its Dances w/ Wolves, Lst of duh Mohicans,Tarzan, Sheena of duh Jungle, xcpt w/ spcl fx. Same, old, hackneyed, colonial theme: Disaffctd westerner lives w/ natives/ savages & over nite becomes better @ doing wht duh poor, dumb savages hv bn doing since time in memorial and ultimately becoming leader of said dumb savages. If u thnk Avatar is gr8, u probably thnk antebellum South was utopia for plantation workers b/c deyz got free room & board. March 3, 2010 at 3:47pm

Alejandra i don't understand the correlation to those movies. i thought it was a great and timely film. reflective of what global and regional hegemons have done for centuries on end. maybe one day people will get the message that it's not cool to be an a**hole as was clearly highlighted, in my opinion, by one of the last lines in the film about the humans going back to their dying earth (the world we are destroying for no other reason but greed).

well that is my analysis of it, anyway.. :p
March 3, 2010 at 3:56pm

Guajiro OK obviously you did not see the 3D version.. it is much different from anything you guys are saying when you see it in 3D!
March 3, 2010 at 4:09pm

Dana Nuheritage Well Alejandra, let me understand it 2 u den: Tarzan goes to jungle. Becomes better jungler then duh jungle ppl r junglers. Kevin Costner goes Njun. Becomes better Njun den Njuns. Avatar goes to space becomes better Alien den Aliens. Dats how I make dat correlation.
March 3, 2010 at 4:10pm

BOMBS FALL ON THOSE WHO DROP BOMBS

Dana Nuheritage Another recent Avataresque film: Duh Last Samurai. Do u blv Tom Cruise becoming a better samurai n 6 months den any body else n Japan.
March 3, 2010 at 4:21pm

Jessica OMG, you're such a dude. It's the most beautiful movie ever. Yes, the story has been told a million times. But Avatar is VISUALLY STUNNING and PURE ENTERTAINMENT! Moreover, it's a reminder that we are one with nature. Don't make me clobber you on the head Dana.
March 3, 2010 at 4:25pm

Max Sometimes you have to enjoy entertainment for exactly what it is. Entertainment, a chance to either get out or stay @ home and allow your mind to get away momentarily. Hollywood rarely makes movies that are 100% based on our realistic views. Only we can do that. What's good for the goose is not always good for the gander.
March 3, 2010 at 6:00pm

Dana Nuheritage Max does duh mind ever gt away? When movie aftr movie tells a ppl dat their savior is(was) a western avatar descended from on high, *deus ex machina*, thy'll blv it, no matter how historically preposterous the idea is. If it were not so, we shld hv bn content w/ being portrayed only as pimps, hoes, buffoons & minstrels. Y? B/c it's only entertainment.
March 3, 2010 at 8:18pm

Max Trust me! My comments are not an objection to yours, i side with you and your opinion. But for years i've given up on hollywood interpretation of reality. So i take everything for what it is. ENTERTAINMENT.
March 4, 2010 at 7:02pm

Got stopped by a cop 4 speeding, yet he had no radar & didnt pace me. Came 2 my door barking ass if he were a drill srgnt & I was n boot camp. Askd whr I was coming frm & going 2. I askd wht rlvnc is dat if u r stopping me 4 speeding. Den he lockd me up 4 DUI. Prosecutor told me the case will b dismssd b/c my blood alcohol was well below lgl ltd. Pnt of story, he locked me up b/c I didnt act like a trained circus monkey & jmp thru his hoops.
March 10, 2010 at 9:22am

> **Christa** EXACTLY!! Dude you know you gots to be like "yes sah boss"
> March 10, 2010 at 9:26am

> **Melanie** where this happen at?
> March 10, 2010 at 9:30am

> **Dana Nuheritage** Phlly, where u hv 2 sit n jail 18 hours just to b processed and released on ur own recognizance. Most places I know of only take 2-4hrs.
> March 10, 2010 at 9:32am

> **Gene** As a former cop I can tell you that they have good and bad days and this dude was having a bad day...still there is a middle road in dealing with authority that recognizes their authority but pacifies their need to investigate u....
> March 10, 2010 at 10:54am

> **Zell** lol where were u?
> March 10, 2010 at 12:51pm

> **Dana Nuheritage** This cop locked me up @ 1a & I was released 7p following nite b/c I chose not 2 answer questions yelled @ me. I requested the dash-cam footage. Going to post it online. U think Sharpton wld get

nvolved?
March 10, 2010 at 3:40pm

Jennifer the situation could have turned out different if you kept your comments to a minimum. i got a
ticket once because i got sarcastic with a cop. he asked
if i had been drinking. i was as sober as could be but
mad for getting pulled over. he told me he could have
let me go with a warning but because i was rude and
sarcastic he was giving me a ticket.
March 10, 2010 at 5:29pm

Dana Nuheritage Wish it was as smpl as me being
rude. 1 thing I hv lrnd n life, never b rude or belliger-
ent 2 someone w/ a gun, escpecially whn u dont hv 1.
March 10, 2010 at 7:21pm

Hv u noticed dat if a woman's profile pic is a group shot, she's probably
not duh 1 u most eargerly want 2 meet n duh group & if a woman's profile
name includes duh word "sexy", she probably isn't? I get so many frnd
rqusts from Sexy Dis & Sexy Dat. Whn I opn their pics, I'm immediately
reminded of duh recent, African-American nominee for the Best Actress
Oscar. Wsn't dat such a proud moment?
March 12, 2010 at 12:32pm

CHAPTER TWO

Spring 2010

Silly Season on Obama Begins

Posted after the Patient Protection and Affordable Care Act passed the House of Representatives.

I'm sending the call out to all true patriots. The Obama Admin must b put n its place. Now thy'r mobilizing the FL National Guard to kill all the old ppl there, planning to annex Mexico and editing Southern history books to say the Civil War was not about states' rights butt was fought over slavery. Yesterday's vote marked the end of America's greatnss. March 22, 2010 at 7:51am

The verb to text is like the verb to set, to read, to bet, to wet, etc. There is no need to put "ed" at the end of it to denote the past tense. Ppl, please stop saying u "texted" someone. It sounds stupid. It's abundantly clear in context whether u r talking abt the past or present. First "at" (As n

Where u at?. As opposed to: Where r u?) became a verb, now this. My ears can't take it.
March 24, 2010 at 12:59pm

> Tricia thank you...i had this same discussion with an english prof and she said u are supposed to add the "ed" at the end...it sounds ridiculous but i wasnt about to argue with a professor. I'm so glas somebody else is in my camp :-)
> March 24, 2010 at 1:02pm

> Dana Nuheritage B/c ppl hv a bunch of letters behind their last name dsn't mean thy know from shinola.
> March 24, 2010 at 1:15pm

> Christen actually that sounds better than "i text him or her."..texted just sounds RIGHT.
> March 24, 2010 at 1:20pm

> Dana Nuheritage Poe, poe Christen. Ur generation has grown up hearing such bad English dat u don't know good English when u hears it. I blame rappers & dat Steve Harvey. U probably like duh sound of, "He wetted his bed."
> March 24, 2010 at 1:29pm

> Jessica I like using the word "texted" as much as I enjoy hearing people use the word "conversate" incorrectly. Improper use is forgivable only when one knows that it's incorrect. Some people just enjoy pimpin words. :)
> March 24, 2010 at 1:30pm

> Tricia I don't know u Jessica but I like u already :-) very nicely put. Although like I tell my daughter who

is a senior, when in doubt don't use vocab u r not sure about. A bad vocabulary can sink u and can make a difference in a job interview.
March 24, 2010 at 1:34pm

Dana Nuheritage I hear dat. Ass I say, "Learn duh rules so u can break duh rules w/n duh rules." Butt dey don't know duh rules. Dey ain't pimping, shot callers. Thy r limping, foul
callers and don't know the word is 'converse'. No such word ass 'conversate'.
March 24, 2010 at 1:37pm

What's the difference btwn a spice & an herb, a buffet & a smorgasbord, (n New Orleans) Cajun & Creole cuisines, a filmaker & a director, salsa & mambo, Latino & Hispanic, a wrap & a tortilla, rap & hip hop, hummus & baba ganoush?
March 25, 2010 at 5:05pm

Melanie are you asking because you really want to know--or u being funny.
March 25, 2010 at 5:07pm

Melanie buffet french term used down south smorgasbord norwegian term used in mid west and north west, Minnesota for example
March 25, 2010 at 5:08pm

Melanie cajun (acadian french canadians and native americans people) creole (french-spanish-native americans and africans or blacks americans -caribeans etc)
March 25, 2010 at 5:08pm

Melanie filmaker---artistic term
director--more technical
March 25, 2010 at 5:09pm

Melanie Hispanic (old term)
Latino (new term) same people
March 25, 2010 at 5:10pm

Melanie hip-hop----more fluff-pop influence
rap--more gritty -political and always has a message
March 25, 2010 at 5:11pm

Melanie tortilla (straight from a grill) and prepared
by abuelos and the grounded corn taste is strongly
evident
wrap--cold ass frozen tortilla made by some guy in a
factory, usually more flour than corn meal.
March 25, 2010 at 5:13pm

Melanie hummus is grounded chickpea-lemon juice
and what ever flavor like garlic tahini pepper etc
baba ganoush has lots of other stuff in it....
March 25, 2010 at 5:17pm

Melanie with the cajun and creole cuisine....the creole
presents more african and caribe influence...however
the cajuns have similar dishes from native americans
influence. native americans and blacks in that region
had a lot of contact so cuisines intertwined.
March 25, 2010 at 5:18pm

Jessica You making my brain hurt with all these
questions. It's just semantics. Leave it at that.
March 25, 2010 at 6:49pm

Dana Nuheritage Melanie, so u looked at Wikipedia
butt u hvnt told me anything. Those were like Sarah
Palin responses, i.e. a lot of words leading to no conclusion. What r ur answers?
March 25, 2010 at 9:52pm

Was watching MMA. Beyond duh blood splattered mat, noticed not a lot of brothers participating. Dats b/c we call it duh "WWFF", duh Way We Fought Forreal, or duh "WTMUF", duh Way They Made Us Fight aka "What Mo Fo", give me ur wallet. Anybody see Mandingo? Not did u see me, I mean duh movie.

[Speaking of porn stars, that would be the perfect career --assuming the person was a well adjusted adult—for someone with no living family or relatives who just wanted unlimited sex and a little money. He or she wouldn't have to worry about disgracing the family name or the ridicule parents might receive because of the career choice made by their child. There would only be unlimited sex. Too bad, not many are on the planet completely alone.]
March 27, 2010 at 3:08pm

Mating mpedes human evolutn. If n duh tone of Beldar, parental units dispassionately said: "Lets..make..application..for..recently..gestated..human..embryo", it wld eliminate 99% of human conflict. We wld den b free 2 f-up wrlds lght yrs away b/c there wld b no sex here. It wld eliminate unwanted pregnancies, baby mama/daddy drama & dysfunctional homes. Identical bra size & male endowment wld end duh udder 1%.
March 31, 2010 at 7:01am

Joined a militia today & will hv my 1st field training dis wknd. Can't w8! It's the Charles Manson Anti-Christ Liberation Academy & Suicide Bomber Institute for the Advancement of Mussolinic Propaganda of the Founding Fathers Against Native Americans and Illegals to Preserve the 14 Words and National Armageddon Hitler Youth Revolutionary Apocalyptic Second Amendment Orthodox Patriotic Front Family Research Center Against Gay Marriage to Preserve the Sanctity of Divorce for Heterosexuals
April 1, 2010 at 10:55am

> **Gene** Dude, they recruiting? I'm down with that
> April 1, 2010 at 11:32am

Dana Nuheritage We can use ur Police training. Espclly, snc members r always shooting 1 another over ideological disputes. Thy hv a 1 qustn initiation: U r askd if u blv whether or not Obama was born n America. ps, u mght not want 2 mention ur Cuban ancestry Gene.
April 1, 2010 at 12:31pm

Jessica I'm sure your status post has triggered alarms bells with the NSA, CIA and MFI and they are probably placing you on their terrorist watch list. Thanks to the good 'ol patriot act.
April 1, 2010 at 1:23pm

What's worse den asking a chick dats not pregnant when's her due date? Answer: Not realizing a MyFace friend recently posted group photo is a family portrait. Instead, u commend him on his volunteer work w/ the mentally/genetically challenged. I've never read such harsh words.
April 1, 2010 at 12:57pm

Y tatoo the name of some departed person on yourself? Isn't that y god gave us tombstones?
April 8, 2010 at 9:37am

Americans hv 2 b duh most uninformed/uneducated ppl n history. There is no such language as Chinese, Spanish or African. Many lnguages r spokn n China. Mandarin is most popular. Generally, 4 evry style of Chinese food u know, there is a language (Americans like food analogies). There r also various languages spoken n Spain. Duh most popular is Castillian butt there r Catalan, Basque and others. Nd I even mention duh myriad languages of Africa? Uhhh, yes I do. Forgot I was speaking to an American audience which was the whole reason for this post.
April 8, 2010 at 3:23pm

Max Take it easy.... some of us are still learning (which in my opinion is a forever process)... I am enlightned by what I just read.... just sayin.
April 8, 2010 at 3:50pm

Zell What's your language called? Afrophonics. Lol
April 8, 2010 at 3:54pm

Dana Nuheritage I speak South-of-duh-Jamesaponics. It's understood only w/n a 5 mile radius of my hi school South of the James River.
April 8, 2010 at 4:25pm

After seeing Tiger Wood's latest commercial, I thought if MyFace ever advertised, T.O. shld b spokesperson. Duh commercial wld b a single, tight shot of T.O. benchpressing n his front yard wearing a singlet. As duh camera zooms n from above, straining w/ the w8 over head, T.O. wld say, "I joined MF cuz I luvs me some me. & did u c my update abt pickles being duh best source of pickle juice?"
April 9, 2010 at 11:27am

Marla What????
April 9, 2010 at 11:35am

Dana Nuheritage Xctly Marla. I'm glad my vision is understood.
April 9, 2010 at 11:48am

Marla What I did not get it?
April 9, 2010 at 2:06pm

Dana Nuheritage Precisely my point! U r so wise girl. I knew I shldn't blvd all dat stuff dey say abt u.
April 9, 2010 at 2:26pm

Kristina OMG Dana, you are still a fool! Pickle juice, that sounds like a line from Zoolander....."Water is the essence of wetness"
April 15, 2010 at 6:06pm

My father and 2 of my brothers served dis nation n the Army & 1 brother n duh Marines. Duh Marine is legally blind n 1 eye as a result of combat. He fought in duh Battle of Khafji n duh 1st Gulf War. Don't tell me I hv no rt to make commentary abt America.
April 15, 2010 at 11:06pm

Wow... Just got back from my 1st alien abduction. Thy gave me gr8 nsght n 2 duh universe. Duh unexplained lights in the sky over duh Midwest last night was their ship experiencing duh equivalent of a car backfiring. Since there's no sound n space, we can only c it. They also explnd dat earthquakes & volcanic eruptions r duh reslt of our planet popping its zits.
April 16, 2010 at 5:05am

MF shld institute a moritorium on members posting trite expressions of wisdom unless thy can adequately demonstrate tht thy r mplementing the substance of their posts n their own lives. I know of 1 member n particular that is so emotionally immature yet continues to post the most hackneyed, banal aphorisms. I want to cut him open & repost dem n his brain. "1 needs 1st a long, green phallus like object 2 bcome a pickle."
Radu Udar Duar
April 21, 2010 at 12:48pm

Guajiro very true!
April 21, 2010 at 1:07pm

Shelly Ummm...what's a hackneyed aphorism???? I want to make sure I never post one!! :-)
April 21, 2010 at 2:57pm

Dana Nuheritage Yo Shell! It's not so mch duh sayng butt duh sentiment. Like duh 1s dat suggsts we shldnt judge others. Dat's how Jeffrey Dahmer found his prey. His victims didn't make judgments abt his ntentions. Or dat if ppl r tlkng abt u it means u r on duh road 2 gr8nss.
April 21, 2010 at 4:34pm

Cpl of new aphorisms: "Duh best way to marry a man is not to hv sex w/ him. Duh best way to divorce a man is not to hv sex w/ him." Radu Udar Duar "Women, u can't live w/ em & u can't live w/ em." Larry King
April 21, 2010 at 6:04pm

The Northeast United States has 2 b duh only region n duh world where u can see a woman wearing a hijab w/ skin tight jeans & a belly shirt. Talk about religious ritual for duh sake of ritual or not knowing y certain acts r performed. Dat's like being a hunting enthusiast, cock fight wrangler & a member of PETA.
April 22, 2010 at 11:00am

Since most ppl don't know if thy r eating healthy or not, here's a simple test: Wht colors do u habitually eat? If duh vast majority is an earth tone or white, u r probably hastening ur death. Just saying.... Don't blv me. Order a combo from McDonald's. I betcha duh colors going down ur throat r white & brown. Eat a rainbow ppl.
April 26, 2010 at 8:46pm

Got a copy of NASA's 3 qustn aptitude tst for astronauts. All rt = genius. 1 wrong = avg ntllct. 2 wrong = remedial. 3 wrong = imbecile. The qustns r: 1) What is the color of an orange: True or False? 2) Is it quicker to the moon or by rocket? 3) If on Gilligan's Island, who had Lost in Space? There r no typos n my reproduction of the test & NASA gvs each applicant 2 mins to answer. Nasa allows no qustns abt duh tst's wording. Wld b astronauts must score a perfect score. Rate urslf.
April 27, 2010 at 10:34am

Posted after uploading the dash cam video of Nuheritage's DUI arrest once it was received from the Prosecutor's Office

Backstory: @ 1am I entered hi-way. Had to yld to a trooper alrdy on the hi-way. We looked each other eye to eye & I merged dirctly bhnd him. Thn I took 1st exit whch was abt 3/4 miles. To my surprise I c him abt 3 miles frm where I exited & he pulled me over for speeding. Yet he had no radar and didn't pace me. N his rprt he stated I was "swaying, unruly & he paced me." 2x n video he admits he was nvr bhnd me to pace me and never wrote me a ticket for speeding.
May 2, 2010 at 7:05pm

> **Jessica** Rat bastard.
> May 2, 2010 at 7:22pm
>
> **Dana Nuheritage** He was profiling. For him it was suspicious 2 tk an exit [duh 1 I alwys take] if u r a Black man riding bhnd a cop. So he made up a reason to stop me. Whn I didn't perform like a trained circus monkey he locked me up. He thought he'd pull me over & find drugs, guns or a body. Yet
> AZ blvs its cops wont do duh same w/ "non-American" lookng ppl. Jessica [*born n Central America*] u r non-Am looking. Nxt time I hv to conduct a citizen's arrest on u.
> May 2, 2010 at 9:05pm
>
> **Kristina** so what happened after the lock up?
> May 2, 2010 at 9:08pm
>
> **Dana Nuheritage** Spent 18hrs n a cold, Philly jail listening 2 duh most ignorant conversations, missed my flight to LA dat morning & became an xprt editing video w/ Windows Movie Maker.
> May 2, 2010 at 9:12pm

Kristina lol..if you had it to do again, would u have been more cooperative with that rat bastard? so that you would not have had to endure ignorant conversations (i can picture your face during those exchanges) and missed your flight to la...but i guess the video editing was a good skill to have...lol
May 2, 2010 at 9:16pm

Jessica Fight the power black man!
May 2, 2010 at 10:14pm

Dana Nuheritage @ Kristina: Duh Supreme Crt, n its infinite wsdm, has said 1 nd not evr cooperate w/ cops. It's illegl to lie to them or interfere n the performance of their duties butt not to b uncooperative. So if I were uncooperatv, tht's no reason to arrst me. Butt 2 answer ur questions, my ancestors gave their lives so dat it wld not b a crime to drive while Black. So, wht is it 4 me 2 b inconvienced? PS, I forgot abt duh $200 4 towing my car, rat bastards!
May 3, 2010 at 12:30am

Flournoy Well damn!!!!!!this the laugh ive been looking for all day!!!!!
May 3, 2010 at 1:27am

Kristina That's why I luv u bro!! My daughter and I watched the video, and now she luvs u too.
May 3, 2010 at 5:28am

Mingo Cuz I got a call from my younger bro telln me about ur ordeal. I see you got a sprinkle of bullshit that life sometimes serves everyone. I can't view the video from my iPhone but I will chk it out later. From the previous comments I see you maintained your manhood and not fold to profiling.
May 4, 2010 at 9:18am

To see video of the stop google 'Nuheritage driving while black or use url below:
http://www.youtube.com/watch?v=Mc-borUONCU

If u r a mother dat realizes dat duh sole purpose of parenting is to raise kids dat r emotionally equipped to be independent, hlthy adults, Happy Mother's Day. If u r like duh 70% dat r creating maladjusted, insecure, abused basket cases, please do duh world a favor and don't hv or raise anymore kids.
May 9, 2010 at 10:45am

> **Shanna** This ain't nothin' but the truth cuz!
> May 9, 2010 at 11:06am
>
> **Cam** i hear ya- but 70%? is that based on philly moms? can't wait to see the percentage for Father's Day lol
> May 9, 2010 at 10:24pm
>
> **Dana Nuheritage** It's based on duh # of times all around this country I personally heard mothers curse, hit and call their kids dumb, stupid, trifling or some such term in public, only god knows wht thy do @ home. Butt ass a social worker, I don't hv to tell u.
> May 10, 2010 at 10:49am

I rarely go 2 movies or wtch tv series b/c thy r so predctbl. Hollywood keeps making duh same movies from year to year. TV only has duh 18tst, gr8tst cop/hosp/lawyer drama or glorified talnt/game show 2 c who'll gt married, win $10,000,000 or an entertainment contract. It's like line dancing: every line dance is a variation uv duh Electric Slide.
May 18, 2010 at 9:12am

Posted by Kristina who has known Nuheritage since middle school and is a couple of years younger than he is.

Dang man! Can you write da regular way (like u learned in English class at George Wythe, Mosby,or primary school). I realize that I'm not as smart as you, and it takes me excree time to read your postings. I must read them because you often have interesting thoughts that you like to express. thank you big bro. kris
May 18, 2010 at 10:29pm

> **Dana Nuheritage** Ize just b trying 2 write duh way u young ppl b doesing. U know how yallz b doing w/ ur ultra hip, hip-hop lingo & neo-txtng spelling conventions. Plus MF alots a maximum of 250 characters to a post. U hv to await my book/comedy/music tour and tent revival to see more grammatically standardized materials. N other words: Train uh caming. Hize u knew? I hurd dem dair whizzel dem blew.
> May 18, 2010 at 11:55pm

> **Kristina** lol..thanks for the laugh dana. what a wonderful start to the day. and you know your friends are as ole as your ole a**...like me....creeping up on 50.
> May 19, 2010 at 6:12am

"Anything we do or participate n can b spiritual if we do it w/o fear, assured of the outcome & in an efficient manner. This includes brushing our teeth, taking a walk or a dump, praying, mopping or committing the most heinous & barbaric crime. Who or wht we glorify n wht we do, that's another matter." Radu Udar Duar
June 9, 2010 at 10:25am

Lately I've bn reading & hearing n duh media duh phrase dat something "changed history." Does duh intelligentsia not know something so fundamentally unassailable as duh proposition dat nothing can change history. By definition! Change duh fact dat Columbus got lost, dat yesterday was Monday or duh Titanic sank. Do dat & u'll b able to change history.
June 15, 2010 at 12:34pm

Thrghout history wisdom (Sofia) was portrayed ass a wanton harlot or prostitute. B/c like such women, wisdom will b w/ anyone tht seeks it. Fools r so for thy choose to b so. No wonder the wrld can't suffer u.
June 17, 2010 at 1:39am

> **Shaunn** U like making people really think, Dana!
> June 17, 2010 at 1:43am

> **Dana Nuheritage** If there was a lot more thinkng & a lot less reacting, the wonders humanity wld achieve.
> June 17, 2010 at 9:38am

It's peculiar how many words n English can mean both their polar opposites. For example, "Raise" can mean to erect or it can mean to tear down, "Raze." "Over" can connote a beginning ass n "do over" or it can signify an ending ass n "it's over." So it is w/ us. Hitler was yet tender to his dog & Eva Braun.
June 17, 2010 at 9:28pm

> **Jet** is this what you mull over in your spare time? i'm commenting 'cause I can finally read and understand your posts. LOL!
> June 17, 2010 at 10:52pm

> **Dana Nuheritage** If u understand it, can u xpln it to me? I hv no idea wht I'm talking abt or duh imprtnc of any of dis crap.
> June 18, 2010 at 12:00am

Kids r duh bst dinner companions b/c u can eat all of ur food & most of theirs & thy don't mind a bit. Adults eat all of theirs & den try to gobble down most of urs, or is dat only n America?

And while dining at a fancy restaurant on a 1st date, what is the only dish u can order, clean all the food off ur plate & not give a negative 1st impression? Sushi....

June 21, 2010 at 11:09am

CHAPTER THREE

Summer 2010

A World Cup Experience

Evrydy I'm bombarded w/ emails frm women I dnt knw dat want to sell me a pill to arrest my balding & make me a well endowed, functioning Mandingo. At least I don't get dem frm anyone I formerly dated. Dat cld rlly bruise duh fragile, male ego. Butt if u r duh culprit, plz take me off ur list. "If duh measure of a man was duh amount of hair on his head, Absalom wld hv bn king." Radu Udar Duar
June 22, 2010 at 8:32am

The US will nvr b a soccer power house ass long ass guys too short, too slow & w/ insufficient hand-to-eye coordination for ftbl, bsktbl & bsbll r the professionals.
June 23, 2010 at 12:05pm

Cam shutup hater
June 23, 2010 at 3:50pm

Dana Nuheritage U knw I luvs all humanity. Butt
wht wld u rather do: Make $70,000 n duh MLS or
$15,000,000 n duh
Big 3. Whn salaries n US soccer catch up w/ the top
professional sports, the US will dominate duh wrld.
June 23, 2010 at 4:11pm

*Posted by Jessica who had recently moved backed to the DC Metropolitan Area
from California*

If it gets any more humid, I may have to take up quarters at Glen's pool
so that I don't dissolve.
June 24, 2010 at 8:57am

Dana Nuheritage Wlcm bck to duh East Coast baby.
I'm sure he won't mind, given u got a new tankini tht
"accentuates duh positive & hides duh derogatives"
(another new phrase coined by Radu Udar Duar dat he
leaves foe posterity). Speaking of gr8 posteriors, let's gt
"back"- no pun intended- to ur new swimsuit. Where
iz duh pix of it?
June 24, 2010 at 9:30am

Jessica It's a monokini ! ! I'm NOT posting NO online pics of me in a bathing suit. I'm gonna call Glen
today so he's prepared when I show up at his front door
step. Hee hee.
June 24, 2010 at 10:04am

Dana Nuheritage Showing up on his door step
blocking out duh sun w/ ur phat @$$ hanging out n
ur 'mono'-kini? Is that a good idea? Is that y thy call
it a monkey suit? [*mono means monkey in Spanish*]

June 24, 2010 at 10:10am

Jessica Mine is the shizzle. It's not a monkey suit.
June 24, 2010 at 10:23am

Posted by Nuheritage's sister in-law, Tracey.

you gotta problem with your 's' key. it's repeating when you write as(s) or
are you doing that on purpose. not sure why but its givin me a good laugh
June 24, 2010 at 10:05pm

> Dana Nuheritage Well go ahead & rub it n Radu's
> face dat he didn't go to a fine school like VCU duh way
> u did & learn how to spll properly. Not all uv us wuz
> born wid a silvuh spoon n mouth butt Radu tryses to
> do duh bst Radu can. Ize b from Blackwell. If u dnt
> knw wht dat meanses, u bedder must axe smbdy. Ize
> gonna tell ur hubby to gt his woman n chck.
> June 24, 2010 at 11:15pm

> Tracey {{{violins playing for poor little Radu}}}}
> June 28, 2010 at 4:46pm

Duh slip dress was nvntd by a wrkng girl who escaped duh clutches of
a crazed john wearing only her undergarments & pumps. She was so un-
nervcd by her ordeal dat she wlkd duh streets aftrwrds for hours n broad
daylight n dat state of dress. Duh moral of duh story: Some good comes
from evry travail.
June 27, 2010 at 2:53am

Y do American soccer commentators feel dey hv to use Britishisms whn
covering games? We play on a 'field' n 'cleats' not a 'pitch' w/ 'boots.'
The score is 'zero' not 'nill.' It's a 'game' not a 'fixture' which is 'tied' not
'equalized.' He's a 'good player' dat's 'healthy not a 'quality footballer'

dats 'fit.' Things r n 'shambles' not things r 'shambolic.' It is a 'pressure' situation not a 'pressurized' one. Puhleez, speak American!
June 30, 2010 at 12:25pm

Waiting to b seated @ a rstaurnt a guy appearing to be a cpl years older thn I strted tlkng 2 me. Later we introduce ourslvs. He says, 'I'm [something inaudible] Mike Thurgood." I repeat, "Mike." He says, " Thts Rev. Mike Thurgood." Was I supposed 2 call him Rev. Thurgood? Folk called Jesus all sorts of things. He nvr said, "Dat'll b Son of David 2 u." Aftr all, I didnt say, 'I'm Radu Udar Duar, he who comes 2 show u how unbibilical ur Christianity hs bcome n 2 millenia.'
July 7, 2010 at 5:02am

> **Micah** [*Nuheritage's cousin with a great number of tattoos*] Your spelling is the only thing unbiblical I see, hahahahhaha!!!! And let the man have his title.
> July 8, 2010 at 4:37pm

> **Dana Nuheritage** Yo Micah, hip-hop culture has mpacted my spelling n duh same degree it has mpacted ur epidermis.

> Ass for his title, nowadays I see so many church ppl calling thmslvs Bishop This, Archbishop That and Evangelist Whatever. What tiltes did Jesus, Paul and Peter insist upon.

> Nah mean?
> July 9, 2010 at 11:15am

> **Micah** Yao Ming
> July 12, 2010 at 9:38am

Posted before the 2010 World cup final pitting Spain against the Netherland.

Rooting for duh Dutch. Spent 4 wks traveling thru Spain n 2006. It was so racist there I got home sick. Was stopped by the cops while wlkng n Granada. Njyd duh opportunity to say, "No speaky Spahny." Duh Netherlands, on duh other hand (duh racist Boers not withstndng), was 1 of duh most polite, tourist friendly and wlcmng countries I'v evr visited. July 11, 2010 at 3:32pm

> **Liz** Wow, it must b nice to travel like that...
> July 11, 2010 at 7:16pm

> **Dana Nuheritage** I'v nvr bn into jewelry, xpnsv cars or living n houses too big for me to keep clean alone. Instead, I've done a lot uv traveling while young enuf not to b on a senior citizen bus tour or cruise. Still hv a lot uv places to hit.
> July 11, 2010 at 7:35pm

Posted after Brazilian player Kaka was given a red card after bumping into an Ivory Coast player who proceeded to roll on the ground like he had been shot with a rubber bullet in a Middle East protest.

Been watching duh World Cup snc '94. Ass qualty of play goes, dis was duh wrst 1. Far ass duh calling of ticky tack fouls, the issuance of yllw & red crds dat changed duh total complexion of duh games that thy were issued n & duh impact on succeeding games, dis was duh worst 1. FIFA stands for: Faking Injury & Fooling Arbitros [*Spanish for referee*].
July 11, 2010 at 11:09pm

2 of my boys said thy were rooting for Spain n duh final b/c thy were Spanish. I said, "I thght y'all were from Puerto Rico & Mexico." Thy said, "We r." So I asked, "Den how r u 2 Spanish?" The Boricua says, "Cuz we speak Spanish." I pointed out to him dat I spoke more Spanish den he did, given he was born n Phlly. Den I said, "I speak English. Dat doesn't make me English."
July 11, 2010 at 11:32pm

Miranda What you say is true. A lot of Latinos who grow up and study in United States are ignorant. That tells you how bad are the schools in our country. Educated people don´t say that they are Spanish because they speak the language. I am Mexican American and I speak Spanish and English. There are a lot of Mexicans, Puerto Ricans, Cubans, Central Americans and South Americans with no Spanish blood what so ever. But they call themselves Spanish.
July 11, 2010 at 11:47pm

Dana Nuheritage U r rt abt dat, growing up n dis cntry can make u ignorant. Butt it's our choice if we remain so.
July 12, 2010 at 12:09am

Miranda what does 'r rt abt dat' mean?
July 12, 2010 at 12:25am

Dana Nuheritage "T.r., t.b.a & t.a.d." backwards. En otras palabras= tienes razon. En serio= You are right about that.
July 12, 2010 at 5:01am

Miranda oh, hahaha thanks for the info.
July 12, 2010 at 12:02pm

MF should outlaw the use of such anacronyms ass: LOL, ROTFL, LMAO, etc. If you have to tell people something is funny, it probably is not.
July 13, 2010 at 2:08am

Micah lol
July 13, 2010 at 9:05am

Dana Nuheritage When replying on a thread , it's acceptable to use them. ROTFL, heee...heee...heeee,

yuck...yuck...yuck, GYWS(gagging u w/ a spoon)...
YCMU(u crack me up)...ONUD (oh no u didnt)
July 13, 2010 at 9:38am

Max lmao...
July 13, 2010 at 10:47am

Cam lmbwao....figure that one out :-)
July 13, 2010 at 3:08pm

Dana Nuheritage Nice Cam! Any1 dat meets u n
person quickly figures dat 1 out b/c u is a PAWG.
lmbbdo! Anybdy got a cigarette?
July 13, 2010 at 3:40pm

Cam ha ha you are retahded
July 13, 2010 at 3:59pm

Cam oh...that was said with my Boston accent btw
since I'm in New England this week :-)
July 13, 2010 at 8:00pm

Dana Nuheritage R u showing dem how to put some
pork n their baked beans?

I'm glad u weren't offended by my last response. It was
inappropriate and I sincerely and profusely apologize
for my language. I should have used the more politically correct and accepted term: 'Whooty' and not
PAWG.
July 13, 2010 at 8:40pm

Cam um i'm afraid to answer that question
July 13, 2010 at 8:49pm

Newt Gingrich said that this Adm is the worst n history. That's like determining the winner of a scorelss game n the 2nd quarter. The only other group in history that tried to rewrite history during the lifetime of those who witnessed that history is the Nazi apologists. At least Cheney has a vested interest n insuring his gr8, gr8 grandson isn't named Richard Biden Obama, or ass posterity will know him: Dicked Bi Obama.
July 15, 2010 at 5:38pm

Many things tht were social stigmas whn I was young rn't any more or r far less so, eg.: Tattoos, divorce, being or dressing like a porn star/hooker/stripper, having a child out of wedlock, living w/ someone outside marriage butt enjoying the fruits thereof, filing bankrptcy, miscegenation & suffering foreclosure. Wisdom & sanity r on the way out ass well.
July 23, 2010 at 9:03am

> **Bruce** Yea, the American "anything goes" culture suffers from a lack of character. What was once wrong is right, and what was right is wrong. A correction is coming. Stay tuned!
> July 24, 2010 at 10:15am

> **Dana Nuheritage** Having a shrink is another xmpl. I dnt suggst these destigmatizations r good or bad. I only point out there has bn noticeable change n cultural norms.
> July 24, 2010 at 10:35am

It's far easier 2 b emotional than to b rational. Jumping around, gettng happy & tlkng abt how much u luv someone or someone luvs u is e z. It's another thing to b pimp slapped & then walk away n peace or empty ur wallet to a person caught stealing from u. Emotion shldn't b exalted over reason. If u ain't doing duh latter, nobody wants to hear abt the former from u. 'U r a clanging gong' empty of discipline & slf contrl.
July 26, 2010 at 12:42am

Penny Call me later and give me the details!
July 26, 2010 at 8:35am

Dana Nuheritage Ain't nothing Penneth. Saw a gospel choir perform dis wknd. Wasn't sure if I was watching a gospel concert or a sumo wrestling match. I wonder if Jesus was conducting, wld he hv bn trampled to death if I threw a pork chop on stage.
July 26, 2010 at 9:23am

Posted after the Cincinatti Bengals, with its infamous Dog Pound section in its home stadium, announced the signing of controversial receiver Terrell Owens to play opposite Ochocinco.

New team slogans & nicknames considered by the Bengals for its star tandem: Ocho y Loco, Cincy Media Hounds, Ocho-Stinko, Ocho & The Whine Plus 9 (U better giv'm their face time), Xanax & the Insecurity Complex, Mental & Simple, Stepin Fetchit & the Hatchet (thy'll carve a team apart- their own), Black Face Shuffler & Touch Down Hustler, Curly, Moe & Thy Gotta b n Duh Locker Rm Snorting Blow, Minstrel & Menstrual
July 28, 2010 at 7:33am

A stone age man turned to the leader of his hunting band and said, "I wish there was away to let Ugg (leading another hunting party a mile away) know our precise position and talk to him in real time so he knows xctly where to herd this 11 ton mastodon we're stalking." The hunt leader responded, "That kind of ability is only for the gods. Humanity will nvr hv such capabilities." What can u imagine?
July 29, 2010 at 10:33am

3 wrds n Englsh tht shld hv very ltd usage: 1) Trying: we either do or do not. Stop trying & do. 2) Suppose: Evr ask someone wht his plans r & he says, "I'm suppose to ...." Tht means he's not doing anything he jst told u. He's a tryer. 3) Love: How n 1 breath can u say u love a person & n

the nxt u say u love coffee? If tht is possible, love is a useless word. Radu
Udar Duar
August 2, 2010 at 5:27am

Over summer I hv bn nvited to 68 (u say 69 butt I owe u 1) events where
I was asked to wear all white (Since I wear the same hook-up to all such
events, I now only attend All Dingy or All Black events). All the promot-
ers out there, can we move on to the nxt fad. How abt these party themes:
Conceal ur Tats, Leave ur Piece & Bring Peace, Bring ur Mate, Pull ur
Pants Up & Skirt Down, U Don't Hv the Body to Wear Tht, Do U and
No Muffin Tops.
August 4, 2010 at 10:12am

> **Max** Lmao.... now these are events worth attending...
> August 4, 2010 at 10:28am
>
> **Shatrice** lol..this sounds great! so sick of the same ol'
> August 4, 2010 at 10:43am
>
> **Kim** Get a grip..muffin tops are sexy and you know
> it!
> August 4, 2010 at 11:52am
>
> **Dana Nuheritage** I hear ur muffin top is more like a
> pound cake.....
> August 4, 2010 at 12:18pm
>
> **Kim** My secret is out.
> August 4, 2010 at 12:21pm
>
> **Dana Nuheritage** Just stop baking bread n doze too
> tight shoes of yorn.
> August 4, 2010 at 12:30pm

Wish I had a $ for evry time some1 told me I hd a woman's name. N
response to tht illogical statement, Radu always query: "Would u agree I

am biologically a man? And whatever my name is, since I am a man, it's a man's name? Ergo, by definition, I have a man's name, i.e. a man's name is the name given a man." The unenlightened start scratching their head at tht point. "Ignorance seeks to b resolved." Radu Udar Duar
August 5, 2010 at 12:34am

> **Kristina** Dana, you have a woman's name.
> August 5, 2010 at 7:07pm
>
> **Dana Nuheritage** Kris, 4 ass long ass u hv bn knowing me (since u were n the 6th grade & I was n nursery school or pre k-- tht makes u abt 20yrs older then I b/c u had alrdy flunked a few times leading up to & including middle school; even ass a preschooler I told u not to date Champ b/c he'ld b a bad influence) do u agree I hv alwys bn male?
> August 6, 2010 at 11:32am
>
> **Kristina** LOL..you are sooo funny...lol. Why you gotta bring up the dearly departed.
> August 6, 2010 at 12:40pm
>
> Folks could say the same about the name Kris/Chris... do we really care Dana?..nope.
> August 6, 2010 at 12:47pm
>
> **Dana Nuheritage** Champ passed? Didn't know. Wht yr was tht?
> August 6, 2010 at 2:03pm
>
> **Kristina** Wow..I don't remember, it's been so long. I think I was still in undergrad and found out on one of my trips home; so I guess in the 80's.
> August 6, 2010 at 2:50pm

Resolve ur own shame b 4 criticizing others for theirs. After resolving urs, u can speak to others abt theirs. And tht shld b only to help them to

cast it aside. "A life lived w/o out some sort of shame is a life lived w/o any sort of gain, ass long ass it's not retained." Radu Udar Duar
August 9, 2010 at 12:16pm

Last nght a woman I met out salsa dancing told me w/ a heavy heart that she was afraid for the well being of her 2 sons. Said 1 is a catcher person & the other a thrower person and tht all the playing the field thy do is not good for their health. I thght she was suggesting thy lived an alternative life style. I wanted to know if thy pitch & catch with 1 another. Then I discerned through her Latin American accent that 1 son is a QB & the other a receiver.
August 12, 2010 at 11:48am

Callng the proposed facility near Ground Zero a mosque is like calling a bldng w/ an outdoor smoking area a cigar bar. The current plans r for a community cntr w/ a place for prayer. Butt wht if it were a mosque? There's a church much closer to the epicenter of GZ. Crusaders killed, raped & pillaged thru the Levant n the name of god 'til the 1300s. Yet there r still churches there to this day. Fear & ignorance r the greatst killers.
August 23, 2010 at 12:56am

Some1 dear to my heart said she was going to post the truth abt me: That I'm a hypocrite. I asked, 'Y am I a hypocrite?' B/c said she, I post hi falooting-sounding stuff butt I hv so many faults. My reaction was: DUH! So 4 the record, I'm the greatst profligate, whore monger, murderer, insecure person, thief, letch, terrorist, buffoon, imbecile n the hstry of the wrld & hv disappointed the most ppl evr. Stated diffrntly: I'm human.
August 27, 2010 at 10:04am

> **Shaunn** Dana, I think you are an awesome person. We all are human and are flawed!!! You are not a hypocrite in my opinion!!! Have a great weekend!!! Give that person a second chance and just be happy!!!
> August 27, 2010 at 3:46pm

Kristina Dana, No!! Flawed?....I'm so disappointed!!!
I'm so glad I've luved you all these years...can't stop
now!!
August 27, 2010 at 8:52pm

Dana Nuheritage Glad it doesn't destroy ur faith n
humanity to know Radu isn't perfect.
August 27, 2010 at 10:33pm

Kristina Radu Who? Lol
August 27, 2010 at 11:04pm

Christa How sad u r and I am OUT!
August 29, 2010 at 2:45am

Dana Nuheritage From what or to what might u b
out? & since I pursue peace, sadness nor happiness is
something tht preoccupies me. Thy r determined by
factors external to or outside the control of the individual. Where ass peace is not altered by either.
August 29, 2010 at 9:06am

Heard a pundit earnestly say, "Obama is a muslim b/c he was born so thru
his father's blood line." How can anyone b born a faith? Where xctly on
the dbl helix is the gene for Christianity, Judaism, Buddhism or Islam? R
the masses really tht ignorant? 99.9% r a given faith b/c by coincidence
of time & space thy were born n a country tht observes tht particular
faith. Is god so fickle that salvation is determined by sheer geographical
happenstance?
August 30, 2010 at 2:11pm

Y do politicians alwy say, "the American ppl?" Do thy thnk if thy just
say "Americans" we mght not knw thy r referring to humans butt possibly the flora or other fauna n of the country? And if cucumbers soaked
in vinegar & brine r called "pickles" and strips of potatoes cooked n hot
grease r called "fries" wht shld politicians b called (many vegetables r

pickled & many foods r fried butt those 2 represent the epitome of their respective processes)?
September 1, 2010 at 11:07am

> **Bruce** Repub's say the Dem's don't listen to the American ppl. So, only Repub's are American?
> September 1, 2010 at 11:40am

> **Dana Nuheritage** Xctly my pnt. We hv 2 major parties n dis cntry: The Dim-wit-ocrats & the Re-snub-of-Lincolns. So y don't the Resnubs just say the Dimwits don't listen to "Americans" or "America." Wldn't u know who thy r referring to?
> September 1, 2010 at 12:29pm

Y is wisdom more valuable thn silver & gold? B/c w/ wisdom u can get silver & gold. Butt silver & gold can't get u wisdom. & w/ wisdom u realize silver & gold r ass precious & rare ass the dirt out of whch thy come. So wash the dirt from ur flesh. It only impresses those w/o wisdom, the true poor. Radu Udar Duar, the Cypher Disciple.
September 3, 2010 at 11:40am

CHAPTER FOUR

Fall 2010

The Fall Of Faith

Posted after hearing a pastor tenuously explain how a certain people are cursed for killing Christ.

N a story abt the Civil War wld it b accurate to say, the whites fought to preserve slavery? N 1 abt WWII wld it b accurate to say, the Europeans fought for Naziism? N 1 abt Rwanda wld it b accurate to say the Africans perpetrated genocide? Likewise, n a story where the protagonist is Jewish, his supporters r Jewish & 98% of all major & minor characters r Jewish, is it accurate to say, the Jews killed him? And if cursed for doing so, shldn't thy b blessed for giving birth to him?
March 31 at 2:59pm

Radu observed during his 600 mile road trip this past Memorial Wknd tht any Christian radio network or program w/ the word "Family" n the title espouses a "return to the moral foundations this country was created on." Radu is bemused y any "Christian" wld promote a return to genocide, hypocrisy and slavery. Bemused butt not bamboozled.

September 7, 2010 at 10:12am

I got the 2 wk to do list of tht Quran Burning Preacher:

1. Burn Quran
2. Burn cross n Al Sharpton's yrd
3. Burn White House w/ Obama inside (He's reading a Quran n there, I know it)
4. Time travel to attend Nazi book burnings & burnings of Salem witches & Joan of Arc, tools of Satan
5. Return to present & burn all same sex marriage certifiicates. September 8, 2010 at 2:03pm

"In the scriptures r the strictures with the fissures and the sutures." Radu Udar Duar, the Revelationary Cypher
September 8, 2011 at 6:22pm

World religions agree on at least 7 principles: Belief n 1 god, doing good to others, the eternal nature of the soul (i.e., an aftr life), prayer/meditation, giving of alms, the acts/energy we send forth return to us in kind and development of self control/discipline. When humanity focuses on these similarities & not denominational and religious differences owing to culture, how wonderful this existence will b 4 all.
September 9, 2010 at 7:14pm

Why do women spend hours primping & prepping for an evening out or to attend a social event and after thy arrive, take their shoes off? Then thy spend the rest of the night walking bare foot w/ shoes n hand. Tht look ain't cute! Radu suggests putting ur shoes on whn u get out the shower. If ur dogs hurt b 4 u leave the house, opt for another pair of shoes.
September 20, 2010 at 9:42am

Womn shld b required to read men their rghts prior 2 entering a relationship. Guys ur rghts r: U hv the rght 2 enter or decline a relationship. Onced entered n2, anything ever said by u prior 2 or during the course

of the relationship will b remembered 4 life (especially dates &/or times referenced) & may be used agnst u n any argument no matter how remote the statement's date &/or substance r from the date &/or substance of the argument n which used.
September 20, 2010 at 9:13pm

Radu has finally figured out why the color pink is associated w/ women and the color blue w/ men. The interior of every women's vagina is pink. And that pink vagina gives men blue-balls.
September 21, 210 at 5:04am

Radu's invitation to a baseball game was rescinded b/c he refused to wear a player's jersey to the game. Radu will not brand, tatoo, carve or wear another's name on his person. Period! Radu goes so far as even to avoid revealing manufacturers' logos on his clothing. Hwvr, if paid for such endorsements, Radu will hpply reconsider his position.
September 22, 2010 at 11:13am

Radu has unassailable, scientific proof tht humans evolved from primates: ppl who eat holding their fork or spoon palm facing downward. They look just like cavemen holding a club.
October 5, 2010 at 1:57pm

Radu's only sister born of his mother died of breast cancer @ age 32. Yet Radu participates n no marches or purchases products w/ pretty, pink ribbons. 2 decades snc her transition to the nxt existence, death rates from breast cancer have not declined n any statistically significant measure butt $ generated from marches & the sale of merchandise w/ pretty, pink ribbons have increased astronomically. Where does the $ go?
October 6, 2010 at 12:53pm

N light of the Bishop Eddie Long scandal, Radu wonders how service wld b if pastors followed Christ's example. N particular, Christ fielded questions during his sermons. Note the Sermon on the Mnt, all the questions

he took from the crowd. What wld happen if ministers today took questions while preaching? I think they wld b a lot more accntbl for their actions and words.
October 7, 2010 at 4:54pm

> **Max** And there you have it........ I couldn't agree with you more...... man! I'm so excited, bcuz you took that thought right outta my head. Some church members have bcome sheep waiting to be slaughtered instead of following the shepherd.
> October 7, 2010 at 4:58pm

> **Bruce** I think it's a great idea. In many instances, pastors have become untouchable and won't even shake your hand or take a call from you in the time of need. It's sad.
> October 8, 2010 at 1:52pm

I only hv a few more of those items lft. Thy r green (ecologically) w/ pink ribbons; low fat & burn fat; increase performance & bust size; grow hair; will attract a mate; eliminate wrinkles; tan skin & whiten teeth; will quadruple ur daily MF friend requests; gv u the swag of a lil, red, sports car owner; create jobs and keep ur family safe @ night from Osama or anyone tht rhymes there w/ turning the US n2 France.
October 22, 2010 at 11:01am

> **Dana Nuheritage** Oh, and thy r n 3D.
> October 22, 2010 at 11:38am

> **Cicee Parker** Does all that?
> October 22, 2010 at 6:42pm

America is a plantation where citizens r the beguiled slaves and govt the plantation owner. Govt does its best to conceal just how profligate its living standard is, which is solely supported by the toil of the slaves. For if

thy ever find out, the slaves wld burn down the big house, e.g. the French Revolution. So nxt time u see an attck ad on tv, keep n mind: it's a battle amngst slave masters for control of the plantation.
October 22, 2010 at 12:31pm

>**Maria** Don't you work for the government????
>October 22, 2010 at 7:02pm
>
>**Dana Nuheritage** I do….uhhh….. Govt is the panacea of all ills…..
>October 22, 2010 at 7:47pm
>
>**Gabe** Dana - Is that an original thought process? Brilliant!
>October 23, 2010 at 11:06am
>
>**Dana Nuheritage** I was quoting Radu Udar Duar, the Great Cypher
>October 24, 2010 at 9:18pm
>
>**Gabe** What movie is that from?
>October 24, 2010 at 9:31pm

Democracy is the gap between public opion and official position. Radu Udar Duar
October 24, 2010 at 9:19pm

If u don't like America being socialist, here r a few socialist programs u shld want curtailed: Soc. Sec., Medicaid, Medicare, unemployment insurance, armed forces, USPS, municipal run utilities, public education, police & fire services, public administering of roads, student loan programs, etc. If u don't know these r socialist programs, u deserve whatever politicians foist over ur ignorant, sheepish heads, in addition to what u got during the Bush years.
October 27, 2010 at 6:35pm

Robyn You are crazy!!!
October 27, 2010 at 6:37pm

Dana Nuheritage Agreed and thank u for the com-
pliment. For to be crazy means not to act ass most
ppl do. An most ppl r like cattle n a herd, brainlessly
following the anus immediately n front of their noses.
Butt now dat we know ize is crazy, the question re-
mains: Is I is or is I ain't right?
October 27, 2010 at 6:40pm

Robyn You is right!! LOL!!!!
October 27, 2010 at 7:15pm

Radu's not too up on pop culture. Just saw The Hurt Locker. How'd that
movie win an Oscar? If there's ever an argument to allow openly gay men
in or keep them out of the services, it's The Hurt Locker. Only a woman
director cld hv heterosexual men behaving n such a way. Homo-erotica
aside, In light of the Wikileaks video, what propaganda!
November 2, 2010 at 12:13pm

Didn't like the movie Dead Presidents. Who wants to see a story abt
nobodies going no where and conquering nothing. Butt the life of Vick
to date, impressive saga. Hope he has the wisdom to consider those who
were still there for him 1/2 way thru his bid. Those folks did the act of
love unto him. Radu Udar Duar, the Great Cypher
November 16, 2010 at 12:22pm

Ass he is wont to do, Radu time-traveled to the future & left a note
for himself in the past, our present, which he just discovered today. Get
it? Note says: Gr8 controversy erupts after public elects abundantly less
qualified Palin over African-American & White partner. B/c of blood
splatters on note due to nosebleeds experienced whenever he time travels,
Radu can't tell if the date of voting is 11/10 or 11/12.
November 18, 2010 at 3:42pm

Alzheimerotic refers to:

A. Wilt Chamberlains recollection of his sex life;
B. A senior's inability to find the way back to the bdrm after taking Viagra n the bthrm;
C. Charlie Sheen's penchant for "Always" being "High" & a "Roused";
or
D. All night, nude bingo at the assisted living facility?
November 23, 2010 at 12:35pm

Posted after reading an interview of Luke Scott, a major league pitcher for the Baltimore Orioles and a Birther.

This article sheds light on the Birther movement. It's all a use of code words. If u say ur problem w/ Obama is that he "wasn't born here" and I give u definitive proof that he was [Just listen to his accent. He sounds like he was born here (butt u don't have a problem w/ Schwarzenegger-- whose plausible etymology of his name is: Black Black, the inherent irony of that aside]; yet, u still have issues. Man up & stop speaking code. Just say, "A nigger shldn't run the country!" Stop saying he's socialist, communist, liberal, democrat, too skinny, making death panels, a Muslim, etc. Say what u really think, 'A nigger shldn't run the country butt some of my best friends r Black'.
December 8, 2010 at 2:43pm

Bumped into Asian actor Reggie Lee close to Chinatown n Philly. When I lived n LA, bumped into actors the way u bump into politicians n DC. Xcpt w/ actors u want to ask, "R u really like ur character on t.v.?" Butt w/ politicians u want to ask, "Do u really believe that crap u espouse on t.v.?"

He seemed surprised that I recognized him so close to Chinatown (Does that make him a racist?). Was surprised to learn he's actually Filipino. Some of the coolest Asians I know r Filipinos. Even though my boy Rich, a Filipino, told me Filipinos r not Asians. Go figure? Butt when u visit a Filipino home any doubt that they are Asian is soon dispelled b/c, like all Asians, they inevitably break out the Karaoke machine.

December 9, 2010 at 10:41am

The essence & illusion of the 2 party state: Party #1 wants to tell u who u can marry, who u can sleep w/, who u can get n a fox whole w/ and what u can put n or take out of ur body. Party #2 wants to tell u what to do w/ ur $, how to save ur $ and how to spend ur $. Butt both want to separate u from ur $.
December 10, 2010 at 4:16pm

Will this season vindicate Vick the way 2000 did Ray Lewis? He played n Mon, Thurs & Sun night, primetime games n whch he showed gr8 poise. Cld there hv bn a better schedule to showcase his redemption to the nation {I wld say wrld butt only Nrth Americns follow the dumb game}? There's only 1 other primetime game he has to win to complete the script. We all need a multitude of second chances, grace, forgiveness & opportunity.
December 13, 2010 at 9:55am

At the mall today heard a man say n reference to a biracial kid, "That's an abomination!" I interjected, "That's not an abomination. It's an Obama baby for the nation."
December 23, 2010 at 6:10pm

> **Melanie** what mall were you at and where?
> December 23, 2010 at 6:53pm

> **Dana Nuheritage** The Aryan Nation Republican Mall of the Rising Confederacy. I was standing in front of the Cracker Barrel across from Denny's.
> December 23, 2010 at 10:03pm

Much abt 'institutionalized religion' (Radu prefers tht term b/c many faiths r held hostage) is confusing. Exmpl: Whts the difference btwn an 'evangelical' Christian or a 'born again' Christian and a plain 'Christian.'

Christ is reported to have said, 'All [Christians] must b born again.' The words 'evangelical' and 'angel' come from the same Greek, root word meaning essentially a messenger. Hence an 'evangelical' is a messenger of the gospel, agn wht Christ told 'all Christians' to be. Confusing? It wld b bst if 'evangelicals' heeded the words of St. Francis: 'Preach the gospel at all times. If necessary, use words.'
December 24, 2010 at 5:24am

CHAPTER FIVE

Winter 2010

Merry Commercemas!

What if US forces n the Middle East didn't dress n the uniform of Imperial stormtroopers from Star Wars (whose garb Lucas based on tht of the Nazis n WWII) butt like Iraqis and Afghanis, a la Lawrence of Arabia? Y shld Iraquis trust men who hide their eyes w/ dark shades while holding a locked & loaded M4. Merry Xmas, Happy Holy Days & Bah Humbug.
December 25, 2010 at 12:54pm

The gvt indicted Vick for doing A, B, C to dogs. Vick, for his purposes, plead guilty. Anyone remotely familiar w/ this nation's criminal justice sys knows that what the gvt alleges & what actually transpires r often times poles apart. Only ppl who know for sure what Vick did or did not do to dogs r the ppl of his inner circle. Anyone else is just repeating rumors.
December 29, 2010 at 1:34am

Dana Nuheritage And if u complain abt his inhumane treatment of dogs butt eat pork, poultry or beef, u r really clueless.
December 29, 2010 at 1:46am

Janet Hey Dana - Michael Vick plead guilty. While I wasn't there, I have read several reports that indicate he admitted that he bankrolled the entire operation, participated in fights, had knowledge of dogs who underperformed being executed, and personally participated in the execution of several dogs by hanging, shooting, or drowning. His property was full of cages, rings, racks that are used to tie down and force breed bitches (I watched a long video documentary that showed extensive footage), and of course, dogs in desperate and unimaginable condition. He was convicted, he served his time, he's back on the football field, and that's how it works - criminals are allowed to move on with their lives following completion of their sentence, but for you to imply that the charges and allegations against him were in some way inflated is deplorable.
December 29, 2010 at 8:09am

Dana Nuheritage I implied nothing. I made statements based on my experiences trying cases n the Metro Area. The gvt often times inflates charges to increase it's bargaining position and ability to force defendants to plea. Vick was not convicted of anything. He plead. I heard & saw the same reports ass u & agree that he owned the property & financed a conspiracy that had ass it purpose dog fighting. Under the law, any member of that conspiracy is guilty of any act committed in furtherance of that conspiracy. So if u & I conspire to rob a bank & I shoot & kill a customer, the gvt will indict u for murder, whether u actually shot anybody or not. That's my point.
December 29, 2010 at 9:14am

Janet You specifically said the only people who know for sure what Vick did or did not do to dogs are those people in his inner circle, but I believe that there is sufficient evidence combined with his own personal account of events to make it so that others, those not within his inner circle, also know at least some of what he did. Perhaps I did infer what you did not mean to imply, but the general tone of your post is one that appears, to someone not mincing and interpreting every nuance of your wording and phrasing, as being generally supportive of Michael Vick. Again, possibly my own inference, but I read it, didn't like it, and indicated why. That's *my* point.
December 29, 2010 at 9:38am

Dana Nuheritage I am generally supportive of Vick & any other human that genuinely accepts responsibility for his or her actions. The reason I posted the initial remark is b/c n the past cpl of days I'v heard ppl list a litany of acts committed by Vick tht weren't even n the ndictmnt (which I actually read online when it 1st came out). Acts that, if he did commit, how cld they knw abt them.
December 29, 2010 at 10:23am

Janet I'm supportive of people who generally accept responsibility for their actions, too (he did some reprehensible stuff though - tough for me to forgive as a pit bull lover/owner).
December 29, 2010 at 10:31am

Christa I'm with Janet!
December 29, 2010 at 10:45am

Dana Nuheritage I love dogs the way I love horses, birds, fish and other wildlife. I love them butt dont

want to live n a house w/ them. That attitude may inform my opinion.
December 29, 2010 at 2:23pm

Posted after the hapless Dallas Cowboys, whose owner fired the coach mid-season, mounted a touchdown scoring, dramatice drive in the final minutes to end their season at 6-10 and defeated the Philadelphia Eagles. The Eagles had already secured homefield advantage through the playoffs and the Cowboys' season would be over after this meaningless, road game. The Eagels benched their starters and fielded a team comprised entirely of second string players. Even still, the dying minutes of the game were a metaphor for what desperate men will do to survive.

I'm no ad exec for the NFL butt for a meaningless game btwn scrubs, Dlls @ Phlly was 1 of the most dramatic games evr wtnssd. The mpct & ramifications of tht game reflect the direction football(N America) [aka Gridiron(Austrlia), American football(UK), etc] will take thru this century & acknowledges its origins more than a century ago.
January 3, 2011 at 7:50am

> **Zell** Yes Cowboys!!!! Divisional games always matter!!! Lol for the true fan!!!!! Philly struggling going in. One and done in the playoffs most likely although I would like to see them in the Bowl!!!!
> January 3, 2011 at 11:22am

> **Dana Nuheritage** Phlly has 2 tuff defenses to get thru. Butt n their favor, they r home games agnst teams they alrdy played agnst.
> January 3, 2011 at 11:28am

> **Dana Nuheritage** The interesting thing abt Dallas @ Phlly is how increasingly the game is becoming abt speed & skill. Football is becoming more like soccer & soccer is becoming more like football. Owners know that the only way they can have an 18 game season & compete worldwide w/ soccer &

bsktbll is to take a lot of the violence/big hits out of the game. The human body can't take the mpact @ the skill positions.
January 3, 2011 at 11:32am

Dana Nuheritage Also interesting was how Dallas players mounted that come back. The players had nothing to play for regarding the season butt all to play for concerning their future in football, i.e. their livelihoods. That's some serious motivating snizzit.
January 3, 2011 at 11:35am

Zell Lol well it's all about positioning yourself favorably in the eyes of the new coach, Garrett. Jerry gonna keep him!!! Not sure if he s the one. Though.
January 3, 2011 at 12:01pm

Dana Nuheritage Did u c Garret shove Witten after he caught the touchdown? It was like frat house, rough housing. Not sure Witten thought it was funny.
January 3, 211 at 12:49pm

An engineer used to b a nerd w/ a crew cut n a pair of horn-rimmed glasses, short-sleeved, white shirt w/ a pocket protector who used a slide rule to build tangible things. Now an engineer is an acneed face, grunge kid w/ shoulder length hair riding a skateboard that works w/ '0's & '1's to construct virtual matter n cyberspace who says 'like' every other word. No wonder no one knows how the internet works.
January 5, 2011 at 9:53am

My quest is ended. I'v determind the keys to contentmnt: Thy r a BMI of .99 or less, dyed blond hair (naturl blonds r not ass hppy so thy dye theirs black) & owning a sports car. I came to this epiphany thru a dream where Christ, Buddha & Mohamed star n Fast & the Furious X, Race to Nirvana. Brad Pitt played JC, Johny Depp Mohamed & The Situation was Buddha. I say no more abt the dream for fear of a fatwa & xcomunicatn.

January 6, 2011 at 11:24am

Today I learned of a newly recognized, adolescent, mental disorder: O.D.D. Stands for Oppositional Defiance Disorder. It renders kids incapable of obedience & showing respect. I think a stiff rod might b a compatible home therapy for ODD.

January 11, 2011 at 11:40am

Gregory YOU JUST NEED TOO STOP, BUT YOU ARE SO RIGHT. WHEN I WAS GROWING UP I GOT THAT ROD LIKE I WAS A RUNNAWAY SLAVE.

January 11, 2011 at 11:47am

Max Yup. You know what they say "Spare the Rod, spoil the child."... Marley has already been told of the Rod, she'll meet it one day.

January 11, 2011 at 12:14pm

Paula Exactly!!! Heard of it a year or so ago while working with an undisciplined boy. I did not agree nor let up on him and he did respond, until "they" gave up. When you take discipline out this is what you get. Everything can't be a feel good moment.

January 11, 2011 at 2:36pm

Kathy Hey Hey... Nothing a good old fashion piece of leather won't cure. Matta Fact, your Ma Ma, Grand Daddy, Daddy, Aunt and Uncles demonstrated how it works on All of Us! I say, pass down that tradition. What say Ye?

January 1, 20111 at 2:47pm

Dana Nuheritage I say if it's done out of love, not n anger, and doesn't leave any permanent marks or break any bones, give 'em a wack for me.

MERRY COMMERCEMAS!

January 11, 2011 at 2:50pm

Kathy I don't know what version of the Bible you guy's have but my version, the Good Old King James Version (some ppl may not understand some parts but, this part is clear), Beat them for they will not Die!!!!! (Proverbs 23:13 kjv)
As a note, do not do this when you are angry. Wait until you have time to clam down. Explain why you are about to give them shock treatment, then administer!
January 11, 2011 at 2:56pm

Dana Nuheritage ROD stands for: Rear-end Obliteration Device. Give 'em 1 for me.
January 11, 2011 at 3:18pm

Bo so true - give them a wack, and all these "so called" diseases will be cured, very fast lol
January 11, 2011 at 9:44pm

Wanda This world has provided a diagnosis for EVERYTHING!! No one has to be accountable for their actions anymore. Sad!
January 12, 2011 at 1:27pm

Dana Nuheritage Good point Wandoo. Here r a few more diagnoses thy shld add to the recognized list: Low Assertiveness & Zeal In Employment Acquisition And Retention Syndrome (LAZIE ARS); Compulsive Refusal to Accept Counsel, Knowledge or Heed Elders' Directives (CRACK HED); Dramatic Refusal Of Prioritization Or Understanding Technology (DROP OUT) which may all lead to lead to Juvenile Erotic Rewards Compulsion & Obsessive Fondling Fixation (JERC OFF).
January 15, 2011 at 2:35am

Posted during a time in American history when anything may be politicized, even time itself. The most galling thing is that during this season of political posturing each party claims to speak for the 'true' American people and some politicians advance the most tenous arguments in support of the most indefensible positions. The purpose is to maintain power by promoting fear so people act against their own self-interest. But the attack dog may savage his owner someday. Rep. Gabrielle Giifords shooter feared the government was controlling grammar.

The overwhelming sentiment of the American ppl is against Daylight Savings Time. The vast majority that is negatively impacted by Seasonal Affected Disorders Syndrome proves the mandate to end DST. We, the true party of real Americans, will immediately seek to effect change & pass new legislation prohibiting the manufacture or sale of any time measurement device or chronometer that is able to retard time, i.e. clocks that can b turned an hour ahead or back and kills jobs n America.
January 19, 2011 at 11:42am

> **Melanie** I suffer from S.A.D.S.
> January 19, 2011 at 12:07pm
>
> **Dana Nuheritage** Tht's xctly the point. The American ppl deserve clocks that can't b altered. Changing time kills jobs. U want jobs don't u and to b kept safe from the evildoers that do evil to u? That's the only way to cure SADS. The party that represents the real America, loves god & knows that peace comes only thru strength. It is the only party working to create jobs, find terrorist & cure SADs.
> January 19, 211 at 12:20pm
>
> **Dana Nuheritage** Turning clocks an hour n any direction is why this country has declined and 1 party is killing job growth by not working to pass legislation to end SADS. Real Americans know that.
> January 19, 2011 at 12:25pm

Dana Nuheritage Today at 6'obama pm, when u go to ur healthcare provider pursuant to ur Obamacare policy to face ur death panel, know that by doing so, u r killing jobs. It's not really 6'obama pm b/c government is controlling clocks & controlling grammar.
January 19, 2011 at 12:45pm

Dana Nuheritage And when the unjust cause of Obamatime is curtailed it will be replaced by a far superior means of measuring time that the true party of real America will endeavor to create.
January 19, 2011 at 6:30pm

Just read the GOP (God-fearing Orthodox Patriots) lead House to propose a constitutional amendment proscribing 1) Gay Marriage 2) Abortion 3) Medicinal Cannabis 4) Flag Burning 5) Obamacare 6) Tourism to Cuba & instituting 7) the Pledge of Allegiance n public schools & 8) displaying the X Commandments n all federal ofc bldngs.
January 20, 2011 at 11:04am

Dana Nuheritage Since even the closeted atheists n the GOP recognize that the Pledge of Allegiance & display of the X Commandments arguably violate said Commandments' prohibitions against idolatry & the creation of graven images, these restrictions will be redacted. Thus the proposed constitutional amendment will b colloquially referred to ass: 'VIII Is Enough'.
January 20, 2011 at 11:23am

'A kid w/o chores is like a brothel w/o whores; a boat w/o oars; a beach w/o shores; fungi w/o spores; basketball w/o floors; sports w/o scores and success w/o toil. It's the 21st century. Do u know what u r meant to be?' Radu Udar Duar, the Great Cypher from the forthcoming single: Revelationary Rap, Don't Believe that Crap.
January 24, 2011 at 10:26am

Dana Nuheritage Like herpes w/o sores; malls w/o stores; houses w/o doors; camp fires w/o smores; refugees w/o wars; BP w/o oil; music w/o chords; castles w/o lords; skin w/o pores; sluggers w/o steroids; space w/o asteroids, proctologist w/o hemorrhoids....
January 24 at 11:45am

Radu saw 'King's Speech'. Thought it was a reworking of the 'Madness of King George', which was better. Still, it's a great example how fear (n this context, fear of inadequacy) wreaks havoc on the human mind, spirit & body. Stop running from what u fear. Stop. Turn. & Embrace it. It can become ur greatest strength.
January 25, 2011 at 11:00am

Why n 2011 do the authorities still fire tear gas n a vain attempt to disperse crowds of protesters? What mob has ever said, "Ooops. We all better go home. Here comes the gas." That stuff only serves to pacify bumble bees not some guy w/ a rock shouting, "Allahu Akbar."
January 28, 2011 at 12:59pm

Posted after animal rights activists expressed a hue and cry after Micheal Vick was presented the key to the City of Dallas.

After controversy, Dallas' mayor pro tem says, "I only gave Vick a 'fake' key to the city." After all, the real key is the size of the Empire State Bldng which fits a lock the size of Cowboy Stadium on the Kennel of the City. The real key can only b wielded by the likes of Superman or the Hulk. Since Dallas, like every major US city, euthanizes 1,000s of pets a year, Radu thinks it's apropos.
February 9, 2011 at 1:57am

Valentine's Day should be renamed "Bribing Time Day." Radu Udar Duar, the Revelationary Cypher.
February 14, 2011 at 10:20am

The Government's 'War on Drugs' has always been fought within the borders of America. Any military scientist will tell you that if a government is fighting a war within its own geographical confines, there are only 2 possible conclusions to draw: 1) The government is loosing; or 2) It's fighting a civil war against its own citizens. Radu Udar Duar, the Revelationary Cypher
February 18, 2011 at 12:30pm

Posted after hearing actor Charlene Sheen's response to a reporter who asked Sheen if he was bipolar.

Today Radu ends 25+ years of rumors, conjecture & speculation about his sexuality. Those close to Radu know his intimate predilections. However, persons not close to Radu or who became distant, mouthed inaccurate rumors. This preoccupation amuses Radu; b/c, what difference does it make n ur life what attracts Radu. Butt never the less, Radu announces he is Bi: Bi-Winning!
March 1, 2011 at 9:55am

> **Kristina** Who Cares!!! I've loved u since 6 grade my brotha!!!!
> March 1, 2011 at 10:02am

> **Kristina** Bi the way...I heard the rumor for the 1st time last year!!! again Who Cares!!!
> March 1, 2011 at 10:03am

> **Dana Nuheritage** Guess u missed the Charlie Sheen interview.
> March 1, 2011 at 10:40am

The way we look back on ppl of the 17th, 18th, 19th & 20th cents & r aghast tht many of thm bathed infrequently, used laudanum (an opium derivative, i.e. liquid heroin) the way we use mouthwash , snorted cocaine the way we chew gum, saw vegetables ass something for the poor & warred against ppl solely b/c thy chose a different political or religious system. Posterity will say of us, 'Thy drank tht much soda instead of water, that's how thy elected their president and allowed their politicians to b bought and sold?'

March 1, 2011 at 9:24pm

CHAPTER SIX

Spring 2011

Obama Gets Trump Slapped

Donald Trump may run for President in 2012, the only viable candidate less qualified than Palin. If he wins, Kim Kardashian's new single shld win the Grammy n 2012; Charlie Sheen should b Drug Czar; Khadaffy shld get the Nobel Peace Prize; John Boehner shld win the Iron Man competition & Lindsay Lohan shld win most improved on Celebrity Rehab. Welcome to the United States of Avarice, Affectation & Arrogance. March 2 at 2:48pm

I'm ass interested in the media bombardment of the marriage plans of Prince William & Kate Middleton in direct proportion to my interest n reading ppl's mundane postings such ass weekend plans that don't include me. Which reminds me, changed the toilet paper roll today. Trying it w/ the flap under for the 1st time. Wonder if that's more efficacious for achieving the perfect wipe. Stay tuned MF; results forthcoming.

March 8 at 9:21am

> **Max** I can tell you now. Its not. The only time
> you can get the perfect wipe is when you wear dark
> undergarment.
> March 8 at 9:49am
>
> **Maria** Flap over is better...
> March 8 at 10:44am
>
> **Dana Nuheritage** It's a trick post. No such thing ass
> the perfect wipe, xcpt if u hop in the shower afterwrds.
> March 9 at 2:55am

Radu was asked what he listens to on his Ipod. Radu responded that he
doesn't own 1 or any other individual, digital player. Radu xplained tht
he dreams of at least 1 song a week & tht he hears music everywhere ass
n the matins of birds & the dirges of escalators, which r free. Radu njoys
moving through public w/ his ear-gate unencumbered so the noise of a
song dsn't drown out the music abt him and n him.
March 29 at 4:41am

Radu dsnt understnd wht we mean whn we say we love this country. Do
we mean smthng geographicl, meteorologicl, aesthetic, architecturl? Do
we mean we love the flag? If so, tht begs the question b/c a flag is only
symbolic. No1 ever really died for a flag butt wht it represents. Do we
mean we love a segment of the population, if not all of it? And if we love
the entire population, the ppl here r from all arnd the wrld. So, shldn't
we love the wrld?
April 7 at 12:21pm

> **Max** Ha ha. I appreciate the virtues, opportunities, as
> well as the topography, geography, and the fact that i
> know Radu... lol. Thanks America.
> April 7 at 2:05pm

Dana Nuheritage
Radu appreciates u bro. U met Radu @ his lowest
point n life. U were the 1st glimpse of flickering light
which illumined the dark ascent out of tht dismal
abyss. N acknowledgment of tht fact, Radu wants to
include the song he wrote abt his ...time w/ u & ur late
wife on his nxt CD, 'My Brother, He Helped Me Out'.
But he dsnt remember the chords. He has the lyrics &
used to play it w/ the band n LA @ every performance.
But that was 7 years ago. Life is racing by Dude.
April 7 at 2:23pm

Posted during the budgetary fights that threaten to shut down the Federal government.

Whether u agree w/ their politics or not, u must admit Tea Partiers r committed to their political cause w/ the vigor of the AWB, Nazis, Stalinists
& Khmer Rouge. If only the Dim-wit-ocrats were committed to theirs
w/ the tenacity of Gandhi, MLK or Mandela. If all politicians had the
conviction to do whats best for America, nstead of their reelection, this
country cld really address the 5,000lb gorilla n the room.
April 8 at 10:45am

Dana Nuheritage It's all political theater. The national debt is approximately $12 trillion and they are
arguing about $30 billion. That's like me owing a
deceased man or woman $12,000 and giving his or her
surviving spouse $30 to feed their 4 kids.
April 8 at 11:26am

Melanie as long as masa give us dem food stamps we
cant complain (thats the mentality)
April 9 at 2:29am

Dana Nuheritage Xcpt Massuh doesn't want u to know that most of his food stamps go to those living n duh Big House.
April 9 at 5:47am

"It is always good to forgive. Butt to forget may cause forgiveness of the same transgressor the same transgression." Radu Udar
April 19 at 6:19am

Trump: "I'll b a gr8 president. I hv a really gr8 co. I make fantastic deals. I went to gr8 schools. I'm really smart. I'm richer thn Romney. I hv a really gr8 co. I'm really gr8 @ being the Donald. I'll stop the wrld from destroying America. I hv the highst rated show on NBC. China & Russia will quake n their boots when I tell thm wht to do. I hv a really fantastic co. I'll take Libya's oil." America deserves Trump.
April 20 at 4:57am

Effects of a Trump Presidency:

1 1st lady a former supermodel
2 Casinos cash welfare checks
3 The term 'trump' replaces 'pimp' n the American lexicon
4 The combover replaces the Hitler mustache ass most odious hair style
5 Hawaii is 1st state expelled from the Union for aiding and abetting birth cover-up
6 Bin Laden finally given a stern talking to
7 All non millionaires r fired
8 Bush no longer leading contender for dumbest president ever
9 China challenged to double or nothing for it's share of US debt
10 Enron stock exchanged for US Bonds
April 20 at 2:41pm

I finally figured out Zumba. It's just the latest aerobic exercise craze that combines Tae Bo, Samba, Latin Dance, stripper moves, clown dancing & crunking. I've invented my own exercise regimen. It encompasses the

Soul Train Line, twerkin, line dancing (b/c we really need even more variations of the Electric Side), Denney Terrio's Towel Dance and Thriller choreography. I call it: Just SMAC, Send Me A Check
April 21 at 3:18pm

Brief history of America's manipulation of language: Slavery is called the Peculiar Institution; a war fought over slavery is called a war for states' rights; Apartheid called Jim Crow; Native American and Japanese concentration camps called reservations; "he wasn't born here" replaces "he's a nigger."
April 26 at 12:03pm

> **Dana Nuheritage** Obama can't be president. 'He wasn't born here'.
> April 26 at 12:15pm

> **Max** And according to Trump, he was too poor for Harvard amd Columbia.
> April 26 at 1:23pm

> **Melanie** the term african american...is a way to say black americans are not real americans. ....basically.
> April 26 at 6:18pm

> **Dana Nuheritage** Is that true for the terms Irish American, Italian American, German American, etc., basically?
> April 26 at 8:30pm

> **Melanie** yes,,...but most black folks....native blacks.... we dont grow up in an african culture. and most of us have ancestors who are not just from africa....so....thats why the term BLACK is what i like....it is not a strict definition..where as...AFRICAN AMERICAN implies that you practice culturally african lifestyle....
> April 27 at 7:19am

Dana Nuheritage Each generation we go back, ur ancestors dbl. So we hv 2 parents, 4 grandparents, 8 gr8-grandparents, etc. Given tht progression, anybdy tht can trace his roots n the New World for more than 3 generations probably has ancestors from places other than Africa, xcpt Native Americans.

As for African Americans not being culturally African, that's like saying water polo, soccer, basketball, field hockey & team handball r not similar. African culture pervades the Americas, from eating dishes of rice mixed w/ some bean to Candomble/Santeria/Vodou to obelisks to the direct connection of Osiris, Isis & Horus w/ God, Mary & Jesus.

Go to any celebration of ppl descended more immediately from Africa (b/c at some point all came from there) any place in the world and u'll find the language, clothing, food, music & dances may change butt the behavior of the ppl is the same.
April 27 at 12:23pm

Posted after Obama released his long form birth certificate after a member of his administration flew all the way to Hawaii to procure it from state authorities.

Y new BC doesn't satisfy birthers:

1 Not written on gold plates
2 No burning bush visible @ official White House release
3 Not written n blood
4 Obama still seeking re-election
5 Awaiting 2nd coming of Trump's time-travelling investigators from 1961
6 Muslim terrorists notorious 4 fake documentation
7 Birthers not sure of the proper spelling of the 50th state
8 No mention of rt to bear arms

OBAMA GETS TRUMP SLAPPED

9 No footprint for comparison
10 No holographic photo
April 27 at 10:41am

America has benefited frm the efforts of the gr8test statesmen of the 21st centry. Ass Neville Chamberlain brought peace in his time, Trump solely forced the release of the Obama BC. Im ass honored & proud of Trump ass he is of hmslf. He nxt leaves on a mission to force Gaddafi to take his meds; the French to add more sugar to pastries & the Brits to add fluoride to their drinking water. The Pax Trumpicana begins.
April 27 at 5:48pm

> **Max** The funny thing is while Donald is in Libya, his hair will be in Syria trying to quell that situation. Long live Donald Trumps hair.
> April 27 at 6:23pm
>
> **Max** BREAKING NEWS: Donald Trump's hair was caught entering a LA restaurant with Dick Cheney. Now it all makes sense.
> April 27 at 6:31pm
>
> **Kristina** silly...lol. but i bet the hair was helping cheney walk. it appears to be very stiff and stuuurdy.. just as hair should be.
> April 27 at 6:36pm
>
> **Dana Nuheritage** Since everybody now knows Trump can get things done, Cheney was convincing Trump to have Obama join them on a hunting trip.
> April 28 at 1:36am

Posted after viewing a video montage of Trump set to the music of Stevie Wonder's "He's Mr. Know It All"

The Carnival Barker: "The Blacks love them some me. My crack investigators confirm that their greatest, modern, song writer honored me in verse. If I run (and I may b/c I run a great company) I'll couple the song with my targeted, official campaign slogan directed to the Blacks: 'Greed is good. Let's get paid Dawg.'"
April 28 at 11:38am

Use url below to view video:
http://www.youtube.com/
watch?v=zw_QpRfuHAM&feature=player_embedded#!

Now that the status of Operation Bin Laden is really 'mission accomplished', the President shld have plenty of time on his hands to gather up his kindergarten grades for the Carnival Barker. I wait w/ baited breath for the forthcoming spin that this historic moment will precipitate from Limbaugh, Fox, the GOP & their ilk.
May 1 at 11:59pm

Posted after hearing some birthers remain unconvinced that Obama is a US citizen.

If ur conspiracy theory is based on: Thy cld hv faked it (conceded); thy cld hv lied (sure); a bunch of questions (eg, y now?), then u hv evidence of a conspiracy substantiated by nothing more thn ur feelings. Radu is an advocate of critical thinking. Ass such he is convinced by objective facts. U just sound paranoid. Show ur proof. Thy showed theirs. U just dnt blv it.
May 4 at 4:16am

For those who profess to be Christians: What sayings of Christ do u put forth to justify reveling n the death of anyone? I recall, 'Love/pray for those who curse/revile u'. Is death a thing to b dreaded? N the end, death is harder on the living than the dead. B/c the dead dnt fear death. The living do. 'It's not always the same to be a good person and a good citizen.' Aristotle
May 4 at 4:29am

Bin Laden's crimes against humanity were that he declared war on the US; vowed to attack America; flew 2 bombs into the Twin Towers & killed thousands of ppl all to preserve Islam. The US declared war on Japan; vowed to attack Japan; dropped 2 bombs on Nagasaki and Hiroshima and killed hundreds of thousands ppl to preserve democracy.
May 4 at 9:03am

> **Micah** Could not have said it any better even if I went to law school my self!!!!
> May 4 at 9:04am

> **Jet** The US gave Japan an option, end the war or bombs will be dropped. They chose not to. The US had no option on 9/11.
> May 4 at 9:15am

> **Micah** I personally believe the U.S had many warnings of an attack before 9-11!
> May 4 at 9:18am

> **Jet** Perhaps. But doesn't diminish the fact that so many innocent lives were lost and changed the whole landscape of "security" in this country. All because of pure hatred stemming from one evil man.
> May 4 at 9:25am

> **Dana Nuheritage** @ Jet: There r always options for ppl & nations.
> But let's assume it's ass u say. The warning given to Japan wld not hv been a true warning. Nuclear weapons were unknown to humankind, xcpt those familiar w/ the Manhattan Project, at that time. So if told bombs will fall if u don't surrender, they wld hv thought conventional bombs, not 1 tht wld destroy an entire city n a flash.
> May 4 at 10:09am

Jet Dana, true there are always options. Problem is when nations refuse to take those options. As you know, 2 atomic bombs were dropped. First in Hiroshima and 3 days later in Nagasaki. They might not have realized the full effect of the first atomic bomb, but surely they knew after and yet refused to surrender. Took another 3 weeks after the 2nd bombing for the Japanese to finally surrender.
May 4 at 10:56am

Dana Nuheritage Good point, thy had notice after the 1st bomb. And ass u say, they took 3 wks to surrender after the 2nd bomb. So y drop another only 3 days after the 1st. Japan had not initiated any offensive even prior to the 1st bomb. The Japanese had been contained & American soldiers were just hanging out on ships and bases throughout South East Asia. We cld have just waited them out.

I blv we dropped Fat Man & Little Boy to send a message to the Soviets who were steadily advancing across Europe. Not b/c we had 'no options' n Japan.
May 4 at 11:15am

Jet Waited them out? Tell that to the the Philippines and the rest of the Pacific countries...Japanese military was still very much in force. Think we can agree that war should never be an option. Unfortunately, we dont live in Utopia...
May 4 at 1:00pm

Dana Nuheritage The Allies didn't do what was best for Ethiopians, the Basques, the Jews, the French or many other ppls. Thy did wht was militarily expedient. The Japanese were isolated w/ no functioning navy or air force. The war was coming to an end. As a

Filipina, I'm sure u appreciate tht nukes accelerated tht end.
May 4 at 1:10pm

Jet Can't say that I condone or agree with what was done. The Japanese bombed Pearl Harbor and waged war against all of the Asian countries. The Germans wanted to invade all of Europe not to mention the autrocities committed against the Jews. Something had to be done and at the time, they felt it was the best choice. In hindsight, of course, it was not. Not really sure what we're debating about at this point, but, I'll let you have the last word. LOL!
May 4 at 3:26pm

Dana Nuheritage I thought we were just expressing opinions. Butt here's my last word: U r beautiful when u r debating.
May 4 at 3:46pm

Fearing their names added to the misguided zealots list w/ Joseph McCarthy, John Wilkes Booth & George Wallace,etc.; Bush, Cheney & Rumsfeld claim the use of torture elicited actionable intelligence to locate Bin Laden 7yrs later. If so, y were thy looking for him n caves? He was n the suburbs living n relative comfort for 6yrs surrounded by his wives & children. Spin, spin, spin.
May 4 at 12:59pm

Posted after the Obama Administration released progressively conflicting details on the raid that murdered Bin Laden.

So now we know tht 4 adult males along w/ Bin Laden's wives & children didn't engage dozens of Navy Seals transported by at least 4 helicopters n a 40min fire-fight less than a mile a way from a Pakistani military academy w/o Pakistanis scrambling forces to the site of this raging gun battle. Wow, thx for clearing tht 1 up.
May 5 at 8:16am

Isn't the term 'holy war' an oxymoron? I'll grant u expedient, justifiable or deemed necessary at times butt 'holy'. Ain't nothing holy about war. And the men of god calling for it don't usually fight it. Now peace, that's a holy concept unattained by most on this planet. Radu Udar Duar, the Revelationary Cypher
May 6 at 8:27am

I'm pissed! Trump's not running. I was so looking forward to watching the nation collectively reject greed & ignorance. If Bachmann and Palin don't run, I'm going to be suicidal. The next few months had promised an endless font of political comedy. Now all I may have is Nasty Newt & his penchant for Nazi metaphors & racist innuendos.
May 16 at 1:18pm

Posted the weekend that aged, radio preacher Harold Camping prophesied to be the weekend of Jesus' return (I guess even the Savior lives for the weekend) and that the saints would be gathered up in the resulting rapture.

I'll b glad when this, the last work-week ever n the history of humankind is over. Can't w8 for Saturday the 21st. I wonder shld I turn off the gass or put out the trash? I guess there still b ppl around when the Beatles come out the abyss & start stinging those left behind w/ the amp chords from their instruments.
May 18 at 11:07am

The media no longer broadcast the news butt rather "Info-tainment." Shld we learn during a national news broadcast wht movie won the wknd box office, who was voted off AI/DWTS or who the Carnival Barker fired? To find out what's going on n the world, we seem to hv to watch the BBC or speak French.
May 18 at 11:53am

African Americans r stereotyped ass having made up names replete w/ the 'ah' sound [a phenomenon deep n itslf for 'ah' is the most popular vowel sound n Sanskrit] butt if I meet another Caucasian female named Megan,

Madison, McKenzie or Morgan or a Caucasian male w/ a 1st name tht is traditionally a last name, eg. Taylor or Cole, I'm gonna shoot myslf n the eardrum.
May 20 at 2:16am

Driving n the wee, smll hours of the nght, Radu hs bn tuning n2 the Bible Answer Man phone n, radio show for yrs hearing Brother Camping end each call w/ his signature, 'Thnk u for sharing'. Radu has agreed w/ Camping abt 20% of the time butt is amused by his exegesis b/c he finds most pronouncements xtra-Biblical & is glad to make this statement w/o risking xcommunication, stoning or immolation.
May 21 at 10:28am

Open Letter to Earth: We the 420,000 chosen before the foundation of the World acknowledge Bro. Camping for alerting us to our imminent departure. We r having a gr8 time up here. Our numbers were so few that the world did not take note of our ascension. Having a marvelous time. To those remaining on Earth, watch out for the bumble bees. Judge u soon.
May 23 at 10:04am

> **Max** Hey bro. Can you send a brother a "Pot O Gold" from up yonder? Drop it off @ the end of the rainbow, i'll take it from there.
> May 23 at 10:40am

> **Dana Nuheritage** Dear Earth, god apologized to us profusely. God said it seems Bro. Camping miscalculated by 4 months. So we were all sent back.
> May 24 at 3:46pm

Radu was told by a fellow traveler bemoaning his trek through this veil of tears that after witnessing so much sadness in this world All he had left was his faith. Radu responded, "And All that the sun has is shine. All that god controls is eternity and that's All time." Radu Udar Duar, the Revelationary
May 28 at 2:00am

CHAPTER SEVEN

Summer 2011

Rise of the Teaocracy Hypocrisy

Learned a lot from GOP debate last night. Learned: 1) Herman Cain is ass likely to win the nomination ass Rev. Al Sharpton is to b elected Grand Wizard of the KKK; 2) Obama Admn responsible for the Trail of Tears, WVA seceding from VA & the bombing of Pearl Harbor; 3) America lost millions of manufacturing jobs to China & Mexico due to Obama's love of egg foo young tacos; 4) In a 2nd term Obama wld repeal the Constitution and 5) If taxes for billionaires were cut, gvt was made 90% smaller & ObamaCare hd bn repealed, Camping's 2nd Coming prediction wld hv bn accurate. God postponed rapture 'til after election.
June 14 at 10:51am

Regardless of how long the NFL strike, lockout or whatever u call it lasts, we know who ultimately wins: MLS. Every match I see on television is

played n packed stadiums before excited crowds. Things r a changing n this country, also Obama's fault.
June 18 at 6:09pm

In it's most recent web address, the Party formally known ass the Ku Klux Klan, the Teabaggers, announced that the nation's recent penchant for throwing all white parties is a nostalgic yearning to return to the exciting days when the KKK set the night ablaze w/ midnight, strange fruit parties and human-oyster roasts.
June 24 at 3:36pm

Stuck a firecracker n a steamy, dark brown, moist pile of dog poo covered n flies like an agitated beehive. Ran for cover behind a wall of the house; peered out w/ just my head & upper chest xposed to see the sinking of the Stinkatania. After the blast noticed caca on my shirt. Went n the house & looked n the mirror. Good thing I had my mouth closed, I looked like a smelly, freckled face Peanuts' character.
July 5 at 6:22am

Posted after the Casey Anthony verdict.

Ppl enraged & indignant b/c of a perceived miscarriage of justice based on wht thy think thy know abt 7hrs of daily crtrm testimony summed up n 2mins on cable news. Thts like watching hilights of Lebron's dunks n the NBA finals & then being shocked to learn the Heat lost. Anyone tht didnt sit n tht crtrm ea day to watch the testimony cant make an intelligent decision abt the verdict. To do otherwise is to act from emotion & ignorance.
July 6 at 9:29am

> **Jessica** You hush Dana, you know that girl killed that poor little girl. Don't make me take my earrings off .
> July 6 at 9:07pm

> **Dana Nuheritage** In response to that I'll say the same thing I said abt OJ, 'I wldn't b surprised if she

did it and I wldn't b surprised if she didn't do it.' No one outside of that immediate family knows for sure whether that chick killed her daughter.
July 6 at 9:20pm

Jessica No worries. Karma will make its round.
July 7 at 10:23am

Dana Nuheritage That I agree w/ & we r all subject to it.
July 7 at 10:39am

Christa Finally agreed on something!
July 7 at 3:36pm

The Marriage Vow signed by Michele Bachmann & other GOP candidates raises suspicions 4 me. Y does a document written by White Republicans who don't expect Blacks signatories reference African Americans n the first 2 bullet points? Y does a document that purports to extol the virtues of Judeo-Christian marriage define it ass btwn 1 man & 1 woman when some patriarchs of the Bible were polygamous? Is this 2011 or 1611?
July 11 at 1:13pm

Since Radu doesn't roll like he used to, here's a few of his pat responses that may b used ass ice breakers/pick-up lines that he bequeaths to a desperate male (and possibly female—not that there's anything wrong w/ that) public & the oft heard question they answer [It helps if the response is delivered w/ a sexy look askance]:

> 1. Q: Did u miss me? R: Of course I did. I miss u when I'm w/u. Just think how much more I miss u when I'm not w/ u [Expect this obligatory follow up to this pat response, 'How can u miss me when u r w/ me? R: Ass soon ass we come together (whether for an hour, a day or a week), we draw closer to the moment

when u will inevitably leave. Missing u when I'm w/ u acknowledges that unavoidable fact.].
July 19 at 9:46pm

Dana Nuheritage Pat Response #2. Q: Are u seeing anyone? R: I'm looking right at u.
July 19 at 9:49pm

Dana Nuheritage Pat Response #3. [*For when someone inquires about the free space next to u at a bar*] Q: Is anyone sitting in that seat? R: If anyone is sitting there, they r invisible.
July 19 at 9:53pm

Dana Nuheritage Pat Response #4. Q: Did u tell the bartender to pacifically give me that drink? R: No, butt I atlantically told him it was for ur girl friend. Can u tap her on the shoulder.
July 19 at 9:56pm

Dana Nuheritage Pat Response #5. Q: Do u love me? R: Just..2..more..minutes..and..then..I'll..answer. If that is not the proper context say, 'I love u [then under ur breath] and all humankind.'
July 19 at 10:13pm

Dana Nuheritage Pat Response #6: Q: How can I give u my #, we don't know 1 another? R: At one point ur mother & father didn't know 1 another.
July 19 at 10:18pm

Dana Nuheritage Pat Response #7. Q: How do u think our relationship will turn out? R: We might find out that we can't live w/o each other or we might find out we can't stand 1 another. Butt let's keep doing this tell we know.
July 19 at 10:23pm

Dana Nuheritage Pat Response #8. Q: R we n a relationship? R: Yes, everyone on this planet is in some sort of relationship w/ every other person on the planet. The relationship may only be employer to employee, father to son, stranger to stranger butt they r all relationships.
July 19 at 10:25pm

Dana Nuheritage Pat Response #9. Q: U know I don't drink? R: U have to drink. If u don't, u'll die of dehydration. So down that shot.
July 19 at 10:44pm

Dana Nuheritage Pat Response #10. Q: U r just saying I'm beautiful, aren't u? R: Yes, I did just say that.
July 20 at 10:07am

Posted after the end of the NFL lockout and announcement of a new season.

Bread & Circus Season is about to begin again. Radu can't w8 to hear ppl wax-poet abt folk they don't know; to watch ppl dying from lack of exercise & overeating sit on couches & scarf down hot dogs; to witness fans brawl n defense of private, millionaire clubs of which they r not members and to see those who can least afford it spend hundreds on jerseys that don't even bear their names. *Morituri te salutant!*
July 25 at 10:51am

> **Todd** I'll never look at football the same.
> July 25 at 12:21pm
>
> **Jessica** Who the heck is Radu? You mention him in every post.
> July 25 at 12:31pm
>
> **Dana Nuheritage** Radu Udar Duar, the Revelationary Cypher, Sage of Rage, Purveyor of

Perdition, Iconoclastic Gadfly, Bard of Brevard, Pontif of Montif, Abhorer of Trying & Supposed To, Great Gnasher of Alabaster, Ferryman of Cherry Land, Ankh of Re, Amanuensis of Amun Ra, Champion of Those Working-out Their Own Salvation w/o Telling Others How to Live, Hermes Trismegistus Amongst Us, Hero of a Thousand Faces, Existential Exterminator...........
July 25 at 1:13pm

Jessica Huh? Run that by me again.....in laymens terms pls. Thank you.
July 25 at 1:17pm

Dana Nuheritage ... the Insane Man of Inane Land, the Free Thinker of Fecal Stinker, the Unchanging Truth of Lies Loosed, the Bachmann of Gaymanastan, the Boehner of Lamentation Deficit Land, the Mark Twain Righting Blood Stains, the Samuel Clemons w/o Misgivings......
July 25 at 1:29pm

Jessica You is kwazy! and all this sounds like crazy talk!
July 25 at 1:29pm

Dana Nuheritage That's what was said to Hannibal, Einstein, Zoroaster, Arius, Ashoka, Joan d'Arc, Imhotep, Cheikh Anta Diop.......
July 25 at 1:37pm

Jessica Well, that's what I'm saying to you too. So there. You is KWAZY!
July 25 at 1:39pm

Dana Nuheritage Sounds like u r missing my voice-mail messages.
July 25 at 2:43pm

Jessica LOL! Nope they were crazier too!
July 25 at 2:52pm

Radu noticed a young lady in a shoulder-less, lil black dress w/ a tattoo written across her upper arm n an indecipherable script. Intrigued by what it meant, Radu asked, "Is that Cyrillic*?" Her response was, "No it's Russian."

If u brand urslf w/ indelible markings, shldn't u understand the full meaning of what is written or does bondage to fashion require ignorance?
August 2 at 5:28am

Dana Nuheritage *The alphabet of the former Soviet Union & other nations stretching across Eastern Europe & Asia. That's like responding to the question 'r u from France?' w/ 'no I'm from Paris'.
August 2 at 5:31am

Radu posed this to an assembled group of acolytes, "If while reviewing photos on MyFace of ppl ur significant other was previously involved w/ u conclude that he or she dated some serious ugly ppl n the past, what does that say abt ur present & future?"
August 3 at 11:27am

Radu remembers when u cld tell the quality of a movie by how long it ran at the theater or by word of mouth. Case n point, Radu decided to go see Purple Rain not b/c he was a Prince groupie butt b/c it was @ the theatres for 3 months. Now u run to a movie the day it opens, b/c ur mind is manipulated by marketers, then say it was a waste of money. Keep being a sucker. Radu will w8 to c it on cable.
August 5 at 10:33am

Radu wonders y mothers continue to call adult male children, 'My Baby' butt can't figure out y thy can't get these grown men out the house or to keep a job. How many fathers r calling sons 'My Baby'? Radu was the

last born unto his mother. When referred to ass 'the Baby', he always corrected by saying, "No, I'm the youngest."
August 5 at 10:53am

Radu is always tickled when he sees a 'Reserved for Pastor' parking sign n front of a church. The scriptures he reads say the 'pastor is servant of all'. Ass such, he shld b the 1st there. If he's the 1st there, all the parking spaces shld b available.
August 5 at 1:12pm

"Part of America's problm is tht the average voter is ass knwldgbl of current affairs ass the average Christian is knwldgbl of the Bible. The avg voter is heard to say, 'My politicians said....' While the avg Christian is heard to say, 'My pastor said....' And when the pastors r @ the same time the politicians, the end is nigh." Radu Udar Duar
August 5 at 1:45pm

> **Vann** Who is Radu and why do all three of his names use the same letters?
> August 5 at 4:52pm

> **Dana Nuheritage** For he is the Revelationary Cypher is the answer to ur questions.
> August 5 at 8:16pm

> **Vann** I have no idea what you're talking about. But whatever works.
> August 5 at 8:41pm

> **Dana Nuheritage** Radu Udar Duar, the Revelationary Cypher, the Unmoved Mover, the Uncreated Creator, the Preacher to the Seeker, the Teacher of Meeker, the Confessor to the Lessor.....
> August 5 at 9:00pm

Radu was asked to join the writing staff of the new, fall sitcom tht follows a year n the life of a NYC homicide detective doing part-time security @ a local emergency rm while simultaneously enrolled n a joint degree program of medicine & law @ night ass she pursues her dream to become famous on 'So U Think U Can Play the Ukulele'. The show is called 'America's Next Prime Time Top Reality Search, SVU'. Radu declined.
August 11 at 11:38am

Radu notices a spate of women that choose to bedeck thmslvs n apparel & other accoutrement associated w/ the male of the species w/ accompanying mannerism & demeanor (not tht there's anythng wrng w/ tht). However Radu points out tht 'til a woman is faced w/ the immediate & ineluctable need to surreptitiously adjust the family jewels on a crowded public street at hi-noon on a bright, clear, sunny day, she'll never, ever know what it's like to b a man.
August 12 at 4:44am

> **Max** The funny part is, some of these (wanna be dudes) have contempt for the real dudes. Like its our fault, they dont have the "man kit.".. smh
> August 12 at 9:11am

Radu wld support a Constitutional Amendment to ban Shariah Law n the US if the amndmnt also prohibited a mandate to drive on the left, prevented Sushi from becoming the national dish, banned making any song by Milli Vanilli the new national anthem and substituting a 1,000' statue of Freddy Mercury for Lady Liberty n New York harbor, all of which r more likely than this nation becoming a bastion of Shariah Law. Butt let's keep scaring the ignorant.
August 14 at 2:36pm

> **Barbra** You mean scaring the "no-think-ems?"
> August 14 at 6:00pm

In a recent survey many Tea Baggers described themselves ass Christian Conservative/Fundamentalist, Bible believing, anti-immigration, etc. That strikes Radu ass odd given the command to 'treat the alien living w/ u as native born' (Lev. 19:33); 'do not mistreat an alien or oppress him' (Ex 22:21) a command & sentiment recurring n the Bible. To paraphrase Gandhi, "The only problem w/ Christianity is Christians."
August 19 at 2:01pm

Elise alien? for real, that word is in the Bible? If so, then I rest my case for Chariots of the Gods!!
August 19 at 3:57pm

Barbra The world woud be a really wonderful place if it weren't for the people in it, and a lot of people aren't "Christians" because they have family members who are. But that's another topic for another day. :/
August 19 at 7:03pm

Dana Nuheritage Elise that's alien meaning stranger not ET phone home.
Aunt Barbra n my lab I'm still looking to isolate the gene that controls for Christianity, Islam, Judaism, Jainism, Hinduism, etc. I'll let the wrld know when I isolate it.
August 19 at 7:45pm

Barbra okay DanaDoo...that sounds like a topic for a ve-e-e-ry lengthy lab study, replete with etymologies and historical contexts from the Hebraic and Aramaic roots, with a little Josephus thrown in for good measure. The "gene" may be found there, though I have not personally conducted the research required to prove it. Just a theory at this point. BTW, I found a copy of the Peshitta. Talk about eye-opening! And being a student of Hebrew language, I am able to read some of the Aramaic. :) What a difference reading in the original

language makes contrasted to the translations. No wonder scripture is misinterpreted, ergo, misapplied, with no, or sometimes disastrous results!
August 19 at 10:22pm

Dana Nuheritage I know what u mean. I took a Koine Greek course and purchased an interlinear Bible so I could read the New Testament in its original form. I got tired of ppl telling me what the Bible said and wanted to read it in the original form for myself.
August 20 at 12:35am

Elise so that's what you say - it is only ur interpretation - I'm going to go for the ET phoning home, but with a bad connection
August 20 at 1:28am

Elise also, if the people who had good taste had money and the people with money had good taste, the world would be a much better place!
August 20 at 1:29am

Dana Nuheritage Then what was the condition of the world prior to the advent of money?
August 20 at 7:34am

Elise If you are talking about cave men, that would be when men would bop women over the head and drag them to a cave and have 'their way' - which is, according to Susan Brownmiller, women having the need to become coy, to get the strongest man inorder to be defended from the rest.....
August 20 at 10:36am

Dana Nuheritage My point is that money has been n use n society for only abt 5,000 yrs, well after the era of 'cavemen'. Human society as we know it has been around for at least a cpl 100,000 yrs, not referring to

cavemen (agriculture is approximately 10,000 yrs old). Therefore, money can't b the defining characteristic of humanity. That's like trying to determine who u r by examining the last 2 days of ur life.
August 20 at 12:12pm

Radu is patiently waiting for after-shocks from his 1st ever, east coast quake. He is sad to report, however, that he suffered damage from the initial quake: He was awakened from his slumber.
August 23 at 2:16pm

> **Melanie** there was a quake around 3 am last year this time.
> August 23 at 2:19pm

> **Dana Nuheritage** Radu profusely apologized for that disturbance. He had been dreaming that he was surfing. His dreams physically affect this and other parallel existences.
> August 23 at 3:42pm

The earth quake has inspired Radu's new, B'more house groove: "It's time for the undulator....It's time for the undulator.....It's time for the undulator (break).........."
August 23 at 2:24pm

Radu anticipates that services will be packed this wknd. There hvn't been so many seeing the intervention of divine providence on the East Coast since the Spanish & Pilgrims came thru w/ their steel and Bibles.
August 24 at 4:25am

The most socially maladjusted child will make at least 1 friend. Butt the most gregarious, out-going orphan can't make a parent. For those w/ ears to hear & eyes to see, Radu instructs tht ass long ass u r the financial

support for ur childrn, STOP TRYING TO BE THEIR FRIEND! When thy become self sufficient adults (w/ occasional assistance from u) then b friends, if u need 1. Pathetic earthlings.....
August 24 at 9:17am

> **Elise** pathetic earthlings?
> August 24 at 9:47am
>
> **Dana Nuheritage** That's an alien reference. U shld appreciate tht.
> August 24 at 9:48am
>
> **Elise** Y shld I appreciate that?
> August 24 at 9:49am
>
> **Elise** I don't know who Radu is either - pathetic igno-rant earthling am I
> August 24 at 9:50am
>
> **Dana Nuheritage** Radu is the latest incarnation of Hermes Trismegistus, he who summoned ur alien friends.
> August 24 at 9:52am
>
> **Elise** LOL - ur right I do appreciate that!! It's in my memory somewhere.....
> August 24 at 9:55am

Radu finished the last algorithms for his MF app which will correlate the number of individual pics (giving particular w8 to the classic webcam, single arm extended & mirror shots) users post of thmslvs w/ their facial symmetry & body proportions to place them on a continuum ranging from Vain, Narcissistic, Arrogant & Self-Deluded, not necessarily n that order. Radu doesn't xpct many to dwnload his app. Self-examination, un-like slf-delusion, dsn't sell well.
August 24 at 10:05am

Pundits- People Using Negligible Data to Interpret Trends. If they had overwhelming statistics to bolster their opinions they would be called scientists. Radu Udar Duar
August 29 at 9:24am

Posted in response to the many postings thanking god for being spared from the spate of natural disaster visited upon the East Coast during the Summer of 2011.

Which son shld praise his mother more: the son she sat n a busy intersection and then left there butt, after she reaches the sidewalk, sprints back to save him from being hit by a car? Or the son who while crossing the street holding his mother's hand drops to his knees, blocking traffic, to thank her for teaching him how to avoid being run over n the middle of the street? Neither, just get up & cross the street. There r a lot more intersections ahead and it's her duty to teach u how to cross safely.
August 29 at 11:55am

Radu is the only native born American on his soccer team which comprises players from Africa, the Caribbean & Latin America. After a recent game, an opposing player advised him to, 'Go back where u come from'. Since maternally & paternally to his great grandparents and beyond he hails from VA & SC, respectively, Radu declined to go b/c the electricity is still out n those areas from Hurricane Lee.
August 30 at 9:59pm

> **Melanie** who is radu?
> August 30 at 10:02pm
>
> **Kristina** Radu is funny...lol.
> August 30 at 10:17pm
>
> **Elise** He can't come to my house either bc my power is also out.........STILL!!!
> August 30 at 10:34pm

A suggestion: When u put ur hair n a ponytail and it doesn't fall, butt instead sticks out like a horn protruding from the back of ur head, don't wear it up. U r a hazard to ppl on the subway & to grocery shelves every time u turn ur head. I almost lost an eye this morning. Plus hunting season is fast approaching; don't go walking thru the woods backwards. It might get mistaken for a deer antler.
August 31 at 5:28am

Saw a marvelous televangelist who described so many wonderful things god cld do -- feed the poor, convert souls, bring about the rapture -- if we butt sent money. Conquistadors said the Aztecs believed that their sun-god needed human sacrifice to stay n the sky. The 911 Bombers' god needed them to kill infidels to bring peace to the Middle East. Were their gods anymore of a god then this televangelist's? 'Help alleviate suffering n this would not b/c god needs our help to be god butt we need each other to be human'. Radu
September 1 at 7:11am

Posted after reading a story about a college student that went to Lybia to experience the Revolution there and the culminating events of the Arab Spring.

If this story is accurate, u have to marvel at this kid. Whether he dies soon or walks this Earth for a while to come, he'll be able to say he lived. He experienced the world. And many of us in America r afraid to leave our own neighborhoods, whether they contain palaces or projects. I'm not impressed by many butt this kid impresses me. Keep living my man!
September 1 at 6:57pm

'What's the difference in a woman being attracted to a man b/c of his wealth, power or prestige and a man being attracted to a women b/c of her beauty, looks or figure? If she marries for money, does she divorce if her husband goes broke? If he marries for looks, does he divorce his wife if she is disfigured n an accident or gets fat after child birth? More important than y u r attracted to a person is y u stay w/ that person. Keep digging for gold ladies.' Radu Udar Duar, the Great Matcher of Souls
September 2 at 5:16am

Elise You sound gay to me! Not that there's anything wrong with that!
September 2 at 4:34pm

Dana Nuheritage I take note of ur uninformed speculation about my sexuality. For the record, define gay.
September 2 at 4:39pm

Elise LOL - light hearted, full of fun and life and love for fellow humans and above all else a great sense of humour!
September 2 at 4:41pm

Dana Nuheritage In that case, I'm a no nonsense, hey diddle diddle, straight up the middle hetero. I might joke butt I don't play. I don't deviate to the left & I don't deviate to the right. Butt I'll keep watching u, if that's all right.
September 2 at 4:45pm

Elise I wish the Big Lebbowski on you!!
September 2 at 5:04pm

Dana Nuheritage Never saw that movie so I don't get the reference.
September 2 at 8:27pm

Shelli ...the difference is "Can u spell drama?" How shallow a person who bases such a serious relationship on what one has or what one looks like..."man" looks on the outside, God looks on the inside.
September 5 at 8:37am

Elise @Shelli - think you're right xcept that there are people who do look on the inside.
September 5 at 2:21pm

Dana Nuheritage She is rt. Humans look on the outside. So r we surprised when they look at the outward. We were warned that they wld. So get ur outside together. And once they see inside, hopefully they will love who we really r there. Use ur outside to get them to look inside.
September 5 at 2:24pm

Elise WTH are you even talking about? Sorry, but there are plenty of people who don't judge a book by its cover - you must be talking about the republicans!!
September 5 at 2:26pm

Dana Nuheritage Spiritual matters must b discerned w/ spiritual eyes. And ur latter statement contradicts ur former. 'The only way we read a book is to 1st notice it's cover.' Radu Udar Duar, the Scribe of His Tribe
September 5 at 2:30pm

Elise Reading involves comprehension, spirituality is comprehended through human eyes and human minds....
September 5 at 2:34pm

Dana Nuheritage And today is Monday. Butt what's the relevance?
September 5 at 2:42pm

Elise The relevance is that there is a nasty undertone to ur original quote that makes me want to defend all human beings especially the women....
September 5 at 2:48pm

Dana Nuheritage Which quote has a nasty 'under'-tone? Maybe I can put it on top.
September 5 at 2:50pm

Shelli Elise, thank God for those who sincerely do take the time to look on the inside!!!
September 6 at 8:38am

Shelli Dana, what does Radu Udar Duar mean and what is that??? (SMH about you.)
September 6 at 8:39am

Dana Nuheritage Radu Udar Duar is known by many names and is many things to many. U may know him ass the Revelationary Cypher, Sage of Rage, Purveyor of Perdition, Iconoclastic Gadfly, Bard of Brevard, Pontif of Montif, Abhorer of Trying & Supposed To, Great Gnasher of Alabaster, Ferryman of Cherry Land, Ankh of Re, Amanuensis of Amun Ra, Champion of Those Working-out Their Own Salvation w/o Telling Others How to Live, Hermes Trismegistus Amongst Us, Hero of a Thousand Faces, Existential Exterminator, the Insane Man of Inane Land, the Free Thinker of Fecal Stinker, the Unchanging Truth of Lies Loosed, the Bachmann of Gaymanastan, the Boehner of Lamentation Deficit Land, Irene to the Political Scene, Katrina to the Meanest, Diadochia of Atlantis......
September 6 at 10:28am

Joseph Goebbels, Hitler's Minister of Propaganda, is reported ass saying, 'The bigger the lie the more likely ppl r to believe it'. Can some intelligent person please xplain how a piece of legislation which has yet to be implemented is, in the words of the Republicans, 'killing jobs' n 2011? Is the 2012 Summer Olympics causing traffic jams n London today?
September 8 at 1:09am

Posted after watching the GOP presidential debate and hearing many participants invoke the name of Ronald Reagan.

Radu recalls the Reagan administration quite well and is amazed by the beatification & mythologizing utilized to describe him & his presidency.

Touted ass a paragon of Christian, conservative values, he was not religious--his wife consulted astrologers to plan his presidential schedule. He also increased taxes & ballooned the national debt. And Reaganomics has been proven an utter fallacy. Butt who is this Reagan these ignorers of history keep referring to?
September 8 at 12:50pm

> **Kristina** I was thinking the same thing. I guess they didn't wanna speak ill of the dead.
> September 8 at 12:54pm

> **Dana Nuheritage** Speaking factually is just speaking factually. And what does it matter to him what we say abt him: he's dead.
> September 8 at 12:56pm

> **Kristina** I"m just saying maan...u know how folks do...saying all these great things about folks they know were hell on earth; but in death, they're praised and worshipped.
> September 8 at 12:59pm

> **Dana Nuheritage** Butt does that work w/ folks who knew the person u r falsely eulogizing? Aren't folk a little more intelligent n the 21st cent then to believe Washington never told a lie or Reagan united the country? Uhhh....don't answer that.
> September 8 at 1:04pm

> **Kristina** exactly...
> September 8 at 1:09pm

> **Max** Though seeing, they will never see, though hearing they will never hear. I was a teenager during the Reagan years, but i was clever even then to know and

i still dont remember him being what they claim he was.
Max I guess "they" exchange the truth for a lie. SMDH
September 8 at 1:13pm

Kristina @Hutson...unfortunately that's practiced much too often.
September 8 at 1:17pm

Elise it's made up the same as everything else the republicans make up in order to sway the republican masses - shame on them!
September 8 at 2:12pm

A close friend just lambasted Radu for being blasphemous to god and insulting to patriotic Americans n his heretical posts. To appease his friend & salvage a friendship Radu, will now only post noncontroversial, inanely true content apropos for MF. The 1st of which is:

Trimmed my toenails, fingernails & nose hairs. Will leave cuttings on floor for dogs to lap up. Gr8 source of canine calcium.
September 8 at 6:22pm

Max You call that a close friend? Sound more like a distant(very) distant colleague....
September 8 at 6:53pm

Barbra Please don't!!... the inanely true content thing, that is. I'm of the opinion that what you do in your boudoir is none of anybody's bidness. Is that a commentary on the stimulating dialogues that occur on MF?
September 9 at 4:17pm

If, ass according to Michelle Bachmann, hurricanes, earthquakes & tsunamis r god's way of talking to us, god has been running off at the mouth

since the formation of this volatile, thinly rock-covered, spinning, molten metal-ball we live on. So ignore Elijah's xmpl of the 'still, small voice' inside that tells us n unequivocal language what we shld do (1 Kings 19:11-13). It's an obvious imposter. If we butt perfect our understanding of Typhoonese & Cyclonese, we wld know wht god's saying.
September 10 at 6:31am

Radu was asked, "Who do u want to win the big football game?"

His response, "The better team." Further challenged, "Well Radu, which team is the better team?" His response, "Isn't that obvious: the one that wins the game." Radu places no greater emotional commitment into that which he has no control over.
September 11 at 9:34pm

> **Barbra** Ah, attorneys and their circular reasoning! Somehow, though, it makes sense!
> Monday at 11:57am

> **Elise** A win doesn't mean they are the better team, it only mean that they won.
> Monday at 5:16pm

> **Dana Nuheritage** U r absolutely rt Elise, case n point. The 1972 Miami Dolphins, the only squad to go undefeated n the history of the NFL @14-0, was not the best team n the league that year. The best team n the league that year was the New England Patriots @ 3-11. They were adroitly sand bagging for 28 years ass part of their master plan to lull all competitors into a false sense of security until Bill Belichick would reach football coaching maturity n the 21st century.
> Monday at 5:34pm

Posted the night of the 2011 Miss Universe Pageant.

The only way I wld watch the Miss Universe Pageant is if contestants 1st paraded on stage n a 1 piece bathing suit. Successive rounds wld consist of progressively more revealing swim attire. The final & decisive round wld pit those n the most revealing suit, possibly just their sash, n a trampoline jump off. Even then the winner wld have to xhibit the utmost grace and poise ass she prepared me a sandwich and beer to be delivered during commercial n total silence.... Oooops, hold up: YES DEAR....?
Monday at 10:05pm

> **Jet** Oh Dana, just because Miss USA didn't make it is no reason to boycott the show. :-)
> Monday at 10:14pm
>
> **Dana Nuheritage** U mean she didn't make it to the sandwich making round?
> Monday at 10:22pm
>
> **Shaunn** U r such a complicated man with ur many personalities
> Monday at 10:23pm
>
> **Jet** Never even got close.
> Monday at 10:28pm
>
> **Elise** he just uncomplicated himself!! LOL
> Tuesday at 8:10pm

Nodded off on the trolley for 10mins while reading a book on the Haitian Revolution. Woke-up to find my laminated, presidential bookmark missing [no, I didn't drop it]. I guess the take away from that is: Everybody in some way wants a piece of Obama. I'll leave off commenting about the use of media before, during & after the Revolution to even then disseminate misinformation which invoked fear in the hapless French public such that they wld act against their own self-interest, just ass today.
Wednesday at 2:11pm

Kira Is there some significance to you always mis-spelling "as?" PS – what about the Revolution does it cover?
Wednesday at 2:23pm

Dana Nuheritage It addresses the events occurring in Haiti, then known ass [what do u mean, misspelling? Butt I digress....] Saint Domingue, n the 2yrs btwn the beginning of the Revolution and France's abolition of slavery n all it's territories.
The similarities r palpable n the efforts of the planta-tion owners', listing n the winds of change, propa-ganda campaign to influence the French Assembly to defer any action on 'the status of persons', euphemism for slavery b/c just like today politicians won't call a thang what it is, until an exploratory, oversight committee is formed to study the feasibil-ity & impact of any future legislation that might undermine the status quo & kill jobs even prior to its implementation.
Wednesday at 2:47pm

Elise obviously, dana has a fixation! lol
Wednesday at 3:27pm

Max Maaaaan! I love how you "school" these peo-ple, me included. I find it funny how they relate Obamacare to job killing. There's so much subliminal propoganda out there against anything this man does.
Wednesday at 3:29pm

Melanie were you reading Babouk?
Wednesday at 6:23pm

Dana Nuheritage Nope. Don't read much fiction. I'm more interested n what actually transpired in his-

tory and details about the natural laws governing this
rock we live on.
Wednesday at 7:02pm

Melanie bobouk is not entirely fiction-! The story of
dutty boukman is not false...
Wednesday at 7:29pm

Dana Nuheritage True. Babouk is a fictionalized account of Boukman.
Wednesday at 8:17pm

Did u see the dramatic video of Brandon Wright's rescue from un-
derneath a burning car after his motorcycle crash? The actions taken
n the immediate aftermath r a metaphor for the potential this nation
has under our 2 party system, not the actions of those who risked their
lives to lift the car. Radu refers to the suited lawyer standing at the
scene who doesn't lift a finger to help butt instead pulled a business
card from his breast pocket which he placed n the hand of the uncon-
scious Wright.
Thursday at 7:59pm

Elise I didn't see that last part - ur making that up!!
Thursday at 8:41pm

Dana Nuheritage I don't know u well enough to lie
to u. Watch the video.
Thursday at 10:04pm

You have just completed two years with Radu. We began with 9/11 and
end amidst the solemn observances of the ten year anniversary of that fateful
day. During this period of collective, somber reflection, an oft heard refrain
is that America is the greatest country in the history of mankind. And
among contemporary nations, she knows no equal. But these unsubstanti-
ated boast raise the question, what are the metrics of America's greatness?

What objective measures have the touters of greatness employed to give America her number 1 status? What facts prove her greatness?

Using the online CIA World Factbook for most, here are a few facts I have found that rationally measure America's greatness among the community of nations:

America is 34th in the world behind Cuba for highest infant mortality rate. American teens placed 25th out of 34 nations in math and science competency. America is 39th in the world for highest income inequality (Jamaica is 38th, Cameroon is 40th, the Ivory Coast is 41st and Iran is 42nd in that regard.). America is 45th in adult literacy of 179 nations. We are 50th in life expectancy. For expenditures on education we are 43rd immediately behind Ethiopia and Ghana is 46th. Of 153 nations, America has the 18th highest rate of AIDS/HIV deaths, sandwiched between Burma and Burundi. America is 89th of 223 nations for highest death rate. Lastly, of 24 nations, we are the 20th most charitable nation in the world (measured by the percentage of nations' Gross National Income given to help the needy of their own societies and international humanitarian aid through governmental institutions).

Here are some categories where we do place #1: America has the highest incarceration and cesarean section delivery rate of any nation in the world. It is the #1 exporter of armaments. We lead the world in oil consumption. America is also the #1 with the highest, overall, military spending.

As I look back on my life, the two greatest periods of learning for me were my sophomore year in college and my first year of law school. As an undergraduate student majoring in political science, I first learned that because something is written in a book or magazine, doesn't make it true. It is important to know who the author is and what the author's purpose is for a particular text. In law school I learned to think critically and to listen to what is really being said when someone speaks, not what I think the speaker means or what the speaker wants me to believe.

My ultimate purpose for writing this book was to entertain and to get others to think critically. Humanity has an uncanny knack for self-exultation. We search for extraterrestrial life by looking for water in outerspace. That is because all life as we know it on this planet needs water to exist. But does it follow that just because every form of life on Earth requires water to survive, any life beyond this planet will also require water?

Similarly, during the Elian Gonzalez fiasco of 2000, I listened as a caller to a talk radio station made the point that the Cuban government had to be exerting some sort of nefarious control over Elian's father when he obstensibly came to the US to exercise his parental authority and take his son back to Cuba. How else could it be explained that the senior Gonzalez would prefer to get his son and return to Cuba over living in these here United States, the greatest country in the world? The caller failed to realize that most people like where they are from. People from New York City like New York City. People from Iowa like Iowa. The Japanese like Japan. People may leave their homeland but it is generally to better themselves in some fashion. Though estranged from their place of birth, most ultimately plan to return in better steads.

And so it is true with many aspects of religion. Some teach that god is vengeful and jealous. If these traits were displayed by an adult, we would describe that person as emotionally and spiritually immature. For just as we search for humanity in space and believe where we are from is the greatest place on Earth, we search for and make gods in our own image. God help us if god is like us. "I'm convinced that the only thing man ever worshipped is himself."

So is America the greatest country in the history of the world? I know it is peopled by people. That's my answer. I'll let the facts speak for themselves.

Think critically, seek knowledge, enjoy life, shed some tears and laugh even more. That is what Radu would have you do.

EPILOGUE

The remaining threads were not initiated by Nuheritage. They are selected ones he responded to. They demonstrate his penchant for intentionally
inciting controversy and, hopefully, self-examination. Also characterized is
his penchant for logomachy and verbal jousting. Being a pacifist, he needs
some means to vent his anger.

*This thread is excerpted from the messageboard referenced in the Introduction de-
voted to all things salsa. DJ Big Pun posted on this thread. At the time of these
exchanges he was a 400lbs plus, local, popular, salsa dee jay.*

<u>Posted Apr 30, 2009 4:36 PM: Rios</u>

I HAVE TO TELL EVERY SINGLE ONE OF U THAT, MAKE SURE
U STUDY WHAT U GONNA TEACH BEFORE U TELL ANYONE
ELSE OR EXPLAIN SUMTHING.

DO NOT CONFUSE STYLE WITH TECHNIQUE.

DO NOT TEACH YOUR STUDENTS BAD HABITS.

FOR STUDENTS: WHY WOULD U TAKE SPINNING
TECHNIQUES WITH SOMEONE THAT CAN'T SPIN??

WHY WOULD U TAKE LEADING TECHNIQUES OR TURN
PATTERNS WITH SOMEONE THAT DON'T LEAD @ ALL??

PLEASE, MY ADVICE IS TAKE PRIVATE LESSONS AND FIND
A SECOND OPINION; DON'T JUST SIT WITH ONE. IF U FEEL
THAT U HAVEN'T IMPROVE YOUR DANCING IMMEDIATELY

FIND SOMEONE ELSE THAT CAN HELP YOU REMEMBER USE YOUR MONEY WISELY, DON'T GET IMPRESSED BY THE WAY THEY DANCE IS CALLED: TIME DEVELOPMENT WITH PRACTICE AND LOTS OF SOCIAL DANCING. DON'T BE FOOL BY THEIR NAME OR HOW MANY PEOPLE KNOW THEM, THAT'S THE LEAST THING U NEED TO LOOK ON YOUR INSTRUCTOR OR TEACHER. YOU AS A STUDENT IN ORDER FOR YOUR DANCE TO PROGRESS YOU NEED TO PRACTICE IT ON THE DANCE FLOOR WITH DIFFERENT PEOPLE AND USE THE TECHNIQUES OR STYLE THAT YOUR INSTRUCTOR TAUGHT U. SO EVERYONE TAKE NOTES AND TAKE CARE [sic]!

Posted May 11, 2009 2:32 PM: Bailandus

> **"YOU AS A STUDENT IN ORDER FOR YOUR DANCE TO PROGRESS YOU NEED TO PRACTICE IT ON THE DANCE FLOOR WITH DIFFERENT PEOPLE"**

What training is "proper" for a teacher? Who trained Yeshua in Christianity? Who trained Siddhartha in Buddhism? Who trained Mohammad in Islam?

Seems like all an instructor needs is the ability to break down movement and communicate that knowledge verbally such that students get the shock of recognition. And if an instructor is not doing that, any student soon finds that out on the dance floor.

The ability to dance in a social setting w/ anyone, that's the litmus test. Just like the ability to defend oneself is the test of a martial artist, not the belts or degrees possessed.

Who care's about an instructor's training? After a # of classes, can you lead or follow anyone, w/ n reaon, at the average salsa venue? If not, don't blame the instructor. The fault is your own.

This stuff ain't rocket science, despite the efforts of many who desire to systematize something as natural as walking. And if you haven't figured it out yet, salsa is just stylized, rhythmic walking.

Posted May 11, 2009 6:09 PM: Nicolita

> **"This stuff ain't rocket science, despite the efforts of many who desire to systematize something as natural as walking."**

Salsa dancing isn't rocket science, ok. But teaching it effectively is more difficult than it looks. Being an effective instructor doesn't come naturally to some people. Granted, it DOES for some and they may not need training. But, I'm willing to bet that a lot of effective salsa instructors have received some type of training on how to teach it. If not, more power to them!

I, personally, wouldn't pay money to learn from someone who isn't experienced or trained.

Posted May 11, 2009 9:31 PM: Bailandus

I don't disagree. Teaching may be difficult for some and come natural to others.

The important question for me would be how many effective salsa instructors have not received any formal training. What training has the mother/father received who will teach a son/daughter the basics of salsa at the family's, annual, all weekend long, Memorial Day Fiesta and music festival? Probably none. That son/daughter over a period of time will perfect this basic knowledge at other family gatherings, house parties or clubs and quite possibly develope into one of the greatest club salseros in some corner of the world. All this can be achieved w/o any formal training, for some and many.

The 2 greatest means of learning are "doing" and "observing." No matter the instructor, the student will only grow in salsa by dancing. And in the absence of an instructor, the student can grow in salsa by dancing.

<u>Posted May 12, 2009 12:08 PM: DJ Big Pun</u>

> "What training has the mother/father received
> who will teach a son/daughter the basics of salsa
> at the family's, annual, all weekend long, Memorial
> Day Fiesta and music festival? Probably none."

This is what I refer to as a statement that tends to confuse rather than clarify. In a blink of an eye this post went from salsa instructors to parents teaching salsa at a family gathering. Why do I even read this crap? Bailandus thanks for helping me exit your existential world of bullshit!

Come back with whatever you want I wouldn't know 'cause I'm not reading this crap anymore!

Big Pun (out)

<u>Posted May 12, 2009 12:47 PM: Bailandus</u>
This message will be sped to you by the universe, since u won't ever read it first hand, "Peace be w/ you."

Don't worry; I'm not offended. It puts me in the company of lives I greatly admire (some I referenced above) not to be understood. Thinking, speaking and understanding abstract thought is not for everyone.

May be we should probably dumb down the messageboard as not to lose any more irreplaceable members. If preferred, I can write about poop.

<u>Posted May 14, 2009 6:32 PM: Crappy</u>
Now, now - let's not get carried away. Only one person can write about poop on this board. And we all know that person is ME!

<u>Posted May 14, 2009 7:47 PM: Bailandus</u>
Going forward, to prevent anymore stellar members from retreating from the MB, perhaps the Organizers should start a "Poop, Bull S@#t and Existential Only Forum." Given that some members are obviously and detrimentally impacted by crap and refuse to pass postings they

can't digest, this will give them a chance not to step in something they care not read. I would look forward to reading your Poop Posts and writing my existential bull in that file, as to not offend the morbidly flatulated.

– END THREAD –

All remaining threads are excerpted from MyFace. When required, a parenthetical set up is provided.

Initiated by Hank after linking an article about the controversy started by a Norfolk, VA fourth grade teacher who conducted a mock slave auction in her classroom in observance of the 150 anniversary of the beginning of the Civil War by dividing the students of color and Whites into two groups. The white students then bid on the students of color. According to the article, the school is approximately 40% White and 40% Black.

Angela Was this her idea of being creative? What's next...some people are just crazy.
April 11 at 10:17pm

Hank Ok. So I think you agree that this is kinda "retarded"!
April 11 at 10:23pm

Belinda WOW!!!
April 11 at 11:16pm

Elaine What!?!?...SMH!!
April 12 at 12:01am

Tammy Makes no sense at all. What was she thinking? Why did she feel this was the best way to drive home the point? Do we do a "mock snorting" session to teach the kids about cocaine? What about "mock sex w/ adults" to teach them about pedophilia? "Out of the abundance of the

heart, the mouth speaketh." Some folks are beyond crazy. At least insanity can be justified. Her actions were just plain stupid. :-/
April 12 at 10:19am

Hank Ok. Ok. I didn't mean to get you all worked up. But you are 100% right
April 12 at 10:29am

Chris Misguided and ignorant best. This woman either didn't take into account or didn't care about the ramifications of doing this to young children. How are they supposed to react? What questions do they ask their parents? Our cildren should know the real truth behind slavery... the horrors of the middle passages, the eradication of our religion and culture... but not at the expense of their dignity -- at any age
April 12 at 10:37am

Dana Nuheritage How exactly was this mock auction conducted? What were the teachers comments during it? What questions did the students have during & after? What were the attitudes/opinions of the students before, after & during? The articles provides none of this essential nfo. Accordingly, unless folk know more than what is divulged by that woefully lacking synopsis, I don't see how anyone can come to an informed and intelligent conclusion abt the wisdom of the lesson, which only leaves emotional reactions
April 12 at 11:50am

Traci This is another example of poor judgement. She was attempting to bring history to life at the expense of these children's long term thought process. Parents must step in an help educate their children. I did not wait for the school to explain slavery to my daughter. Perhaps this teachers action will encourage more parents to have a voice in their schools.
April 12 at 1:29pm

Chris Dana she divided the students by race and had the white students buy and sell the black and mixed race kids. I, for one, really don't need

much else. Knowing how kids can be, it is not difficult to imagine how this can play out... white kid continuing the scenario orders a black kid to do something because he is his "slave" outside of the classroom. What happens next? I know what I would have done under those circumstances at that age...
April 12 at 2:30pm

Hank ok. I see most agree with my initial reaction, but, it may be a tiny, tiny, bit of room for the benefit of the doubt, from the comments!. I just picked up a book today and it had this Nigerian quote in it "Not to know is bad. Not to wish to know is worse!"
April 12 at 4:26pm

Dana Nuheritage Chris the enslaved students cld have organized a Turner Rebellion & beat-up the slavers; non-slave-owning, white kids n other classes cld hv organized to attack those owning slaves to start a civil war n the school; the principal cld have granted the enslaved passing grades b/c of their history of enforced servitude. A 1,000 things cld hv happened. Let's find out what actually did happen before we start condemning universally.
April 12 at 4:30pm

Chris My man, so you are saying that 1) you don't have enough info (when the teacher divided the students by race, etc.) and suggesting that 2) it may not be so bad because maybe the principal gave the "enslaved" (black) kids a "passing grade....." Which piece of missing information would have made that bs acceptable? A "D" is passing, so is that ok? Or would you need to hear that the "slaves" got B's or better? I can appreciate the need for folks to hear more, but sometimes it's right in front of your face. I cannot imagine any circumstance where that ignorant bs would have been appropriate. The teacher is either woefully out of touch or incredibly mean spirited. Period. The last thing we should do is make excuses for him or her. Our children deserve so much more.
April 12 at 10:22pm

<u>Hank</u> Ok Chris. Ok. I hear that!!
April 12 at 10:39pm

<u>Dana Nuheritage</u> 1) For the record I was speaking hypothetically to make a point. Don't take it literally. 2) The fact u don't even know the sex of the teacher is telling. What if the teacher is black? Wld tht alter ur opinion? 3) When I was n school many of my white friends wore Confederate flag caps & belt buckles. From that shld I infer they were racist?
April 12 at 11:57pm

<u>Chris</u> 1. The teacher's sex doesn't matter. 2. If she was black, then she would fall into the "woefully uninformed" category, although -- come on... We KNOW she wasn't black. 3. Yes; or at the least highly insensitive. The confederate flag has never been a friendly symbol to people of color. Friends don't subject their friends to symbols which would even remotely make them uncomfortable... Unless for some reason that friend who is a minority has somehow signaled that it is "ok." Respectfully, the fact that your "friends" wore that crap around you helps me to better understand your position.
April 13 at 6:49am

<u>Dana Nuheritage</u> Ad hominem attacks aside, the Confederate flag has never made me uncomfortable. Don't know where u r from but I grew up n the Capital of the Confederacy & played football for an inner city school. The majority of the suburban schools we played had Rebel related nicknames & their players towels had the Stars & Bars on them. During the course of a game we wld snatch towels off players and wear them ourselves. That's where I'm coming from. I'm not threatened by anybody's flag, cross, idol or other symbol.
April 13 at 9:06am

<u>Chris</u> No attack, brother. It was just an observation based upon the position you've taken and words you used to support that position. My friends typically were not the ones who wore that crap. And folks who did

wouldn't flaunt it around me. Its not about being intimidated. I wasn't.
It was about respect. Where I'm from people know what that flag has
meant to black people over the years. At least that's been my experience.
As I indicated above, perhaps it wasn't your experience -- which would
explain your approach to this issue.
April 13 at 10:40am

Hank What a lively discussion. Thanks all!
April 13 at 12:03pm

Posted by Nuheritage's niece who is juggling school and work.

heeelp uncle radu, lol. ooook so u are right i have A LOT to think about.
and im still practicing revaluating my spending habits...but when did
you have time to sleep and study??? last semester i worked 2 jobs and
went to school. hence my car accident from lack of sleep and a failed class.
now what??
August 25, 2010 at 12:49pm

> **Dana Nuheritage** We find time for the things we
> choose to find time for. Ur grandmother worked full
> time; went to school full time and spent full time rais-
> ing 4 kids, all at the same time. Decide what n this life
> u'll devote time to. At different times, it may be differ-
> ent things.
> August 25, 2010 at 2:38pm

> **Laine Malik** that is exactly why i asked you, :) thank
> you for a new perspective :) ily
> August 25, 2010 at 9:01pm

*Posted by Nuheritage's first cousin, Myke, front man for a popular, cult heavy-
metal, head-banger band and solo artist, after finally accepting Nuheritage's
friend request sent monthsbefore.*

Myke:
Hahaa my bad cuzzzz! I never check my requests. How have you been! You know, I have to credit you with a lot of my success. You taught me how to play what I heard and how to listen. Who woulda thought those small lessons would have taken me all around the world? Thank you. June 25, 2010 at 12:07pm

> **Dana Nuheritage** Ur success or failure will be determined by u [And failure is only determined from the moment u stop thriving for success]. I did nothing butt recycle talent dat's been circulating n our family since b 4 our gr8 grandfather was duh choir director for his small church n Northside. Ur mom showed me how to play Rod Stewart's "Do Ya Think I'm Sexy" when I was abt 13. Thank her. Butt you can give me back my pitch pipe dat u or ur brother lost whn I lft my axe at ur house tht time.
> June 25, 2010 at 12:50pm

> **Myke** Hahahahahahahahahahahaha aight I'll hook you up. You know we was always losing 120omething. Back then.
> June 25, 2010 at 12:54pm

– END THREAD –

Vann:
Think Obama's gonna get re-elected? Do you think that he should? Why or why not?
September 5 at 12:12pm

> **Yasmine** Nope! He didn't hold true to his word. He really didn't do anything besides go on vacations
> September 5 at 12:15pm

Layi LOL. I am glad I'm not the only person that thinks he just says things just because.....
September 5 at 12:17pm

David I think that he seems to be a sincere man and they are rare. I am from South Africa and we will gladly trade for him too.
September 5 at 12:17pm

Tahnee No, but I also think he hasn't done any worse of a job than any President in the past 3 decades either...Seems like all our government does is go on vacations, cut themselves breaks, and make sure there's a great distinction between the have's and the have not's
September 5 at 12:21pm

David I see too that the other party doesn't want to work with him as he would like to work with them.
September 5 at 12:31pm

Brandon anything major things that a president does takes 3 years average to see affects. I think he is a good president but the republicans arent willing to work in his favor. I mean lets face it, he's cleaning up george bush's shit. That's a lot of shit to clean.
September 5 at 12:33pm

David As leaders go, is he really that bad?
September 5 at 12:38pm

Dana Nuheritage Remember where u heard this: Obama will b re-elected and the Democrats will regain a majority in the House & Senate nxt year. Ass a result, u will see major legistlation passed during his last term, tht like Lincoln's, FDR's & LBJ's administrations, will b discussed for generations. And historians will gauge how racist this country was by how so many

politicians were so willing to sabotage & betray their own nation in order to undermine the administration of the 1st Black president.
September 5 at 12:46pm

David At least you have a say, we don't the ANC are the dominant party here and it seems to me that they might be falling into extremism with political people that are on the rise.
September 5 at 12:49pm

David We already know that Malema will be freed of his crimes and that he will continue with his mouth before brain engagements.
September 5 at 12:51pm

Matthew No, because people are dumb and they believe whatever inaccurate reports Fox News tells them. He's taking heat for stuff he didn't do in a nation that can't admit they're still racist.
September 5 at 1:00pm

David I don't think that he is a great leader, though he is fair and amicably accommodating towards his foes.
September 5 at 1:04pm

Kevin He'll get re-elected because moderate voters aren't going to put Rick Perry or Michelle Bachmann or Sarah Palin for that matter into office. They're crazy enough to rally the far right but not sane enough to rally the indies. I think Obama is a sincere guy whose only crime was believing in the system as it exists today, and that he could work that system as a reasonable adult to produce comprehensive change. But no one wants to play by his rules- they're more obsessed with ousting him than doing anything constructive. And

there are more people pulling the strings behind the curtains than we the people are made aware of, so you can't put any blame or shortcomings squarely on him. Presidents aren't perfect, and why should they be? I think he's gotten a lot done all things considered. And this recession we're in? Get used to it cuz it's gonna be here a while. Nothing the president can do about it. Considering who he's up against, I'm probably gonna vote for him again. There's no one in the GOP field that I can defend with a sane argument. And everyone saying, 'all he did was go on vacations,' need to reevaluate where they're getting their news, to be honest. And even on vacation it's not like he (or any other prez) stops being president while they're away from the white house. It's not like when you or I go on vacation and can turn off the phone and the tv. Please.
September 5 at 1:07pm

Dana Nuheritage Unfortunately, ass woefully ignorant ass most Americans r of what's truly going on n their own country, thy r totally oblivious to what's happening n the world, other than what thy see on the evening news, which is nxt to nothing. I doubt if a majority of the ppl on this thread know what the ANC is or what it stands for. Thy probably think it's a sports league of somekind.

The best way to hide something from the majority of Americans is to put it in a book. That's y politicians here can say the most blatant lies & distortions, especially if thy profess to be a conservative Christian (a oxymoron), & ppl blv it.
September 5 at 1:08pm

David There are leaders that are afraid of their own people and supporters too and they feel that they are next to be booted. Obama is not of that group. I think

though that he has needed to tidy up the ongoing mess that we are seeing across the globe as Europe too enters crisis upon crisis. Obama did not run from his, he dealt with it and understands too that the attention span of the average american is rather short. It is going to take more than him and more than the parties to fix the mess.
September 5 at 1:09pm

David Damm, the average american cannot even find their own country on the world map, let alone South Africa.
September 5 at 1:12pm

Dana Nuheritage @Kevin: those who say he spends too much time on vacation shld objectively compare the number of days to date he's taken vacation w/ that of the 4 previous presidents up to the same time n their 1st term, info that is readily available on the net. Butt they won't do that. They'll just keep saying he's a loafer born n Kenya b/c they heard it from biased source.
September 5 at 1:14pm

Kevin Also dana you keep saying 'Ass' in place of 'as'. Not sure if that was intentional...
September 5 at 1:16pm

Dana Nuheritage Hmmm, so noted. Very astute of u to catch that. Butt I'll let u determine whether I was errant or not.
September 5 at 1:19pm

Kevin As I was just saying to another friend, the GOP's fatal mistake was co-opting the tea party movement just because they were anti-Obama. This is politics, the enemy of your enemy is not always your

friend. Especially if that enemy is foaming at the mouth and cross-eyed.
September 5 at 1:34pm

David I think too that there has to be the right person for the right times and we can but hope that he is the right person for a time such as this.
September 5 at 1:36pm

Dana Nuheritage All gr8 presidents were made so by the gr8ness of the crisis facing them. Obama has the opportunity to be gr8. Providence will determine if history finds him to have bn gr8. Butt no matter what happens, n the grand scheme of things, he'll b forgotten just like every other human who walks this Earth.
September 5 at 1:47pm

Travis Yes we can! We will change! What has changed?!? I'm no rocket scientist but I know one thing is for sure, how in the hell is it humanly possible to spend your way out of debt?!?! Someone please give me the answer because I would be willing to give it a try myself...robbing Peter to pay Paul will end this country as we know it and then the terrorists and anti-american individuals will rave at our demise! And they didn't even have to do anything to destroy us...
September 5 at 1:54pm

Dana Nuheritage Travis u have given an xcllnt xmpl of the kind of statements that politicians use to nflame butt which mean absolutely nothing:

1st) Who advocated spending our way out of debt?
2nd) At a micro & macro level, almost every person, business or political entity has some type of debt. It's not abt being n debt butt the nature of the debt & whether the debt can be properly liquidated.

3rd) What is the purpose of gv't? Does it xist not to be n debt or does it xist to facilitate societal living? If the latter, then sometimes gov't needs to take measure to insure the economy of nation flourishes. And if spending money facilitates that, it shld spend money. It's not solely abt debt.
September 5 at 2:14pm

LaTavia umm our President did uphold his word. how about don't ask don't tell ends this month, health care, credit card companies attacking college kids, student loans and financial aid, women's right and equal pay
September 5 at 5:02pm

LaTavia equal pay etc. how about educate yourself on what he has done not what the bigots want you to hear or how about stop holdin him responsible for thing he cannot control. as president he can only suggest legislation and veto or sign bills. how abou you tell those racist republicans to stop railroading him so he doesn't get re elected. they get away with this bc they know many did not pay attention in civics or govt and think Obama is in charge of EVERYTHING
September 5 at 5:06pm

LaTavia but Obama def has my vote in 2012 and there will be many seat changes in congress as well. I'm sure but I want no teapublican running my country. September 5 at 5:08pm

Vann great discussion. but i don't quite agree with one thing that's been repeated several times. i wouldn't generally characterize republican or america at large's hate for everything Obama as racist. i might be tempted to think that they are riding Obama so hard because they want to see a black man fail as President but then I remember that they did the exact same thing to Clinton over a stupid blow job... A STUPID BLOW JOB!! they disbarred him as an attorney and almost impeached him.

Now that's not to say that some of the hate that many on the right have for Obama isn't racially initiated. Just look at Fox News calling Michelle his baby mama and stupid stuff like that and you should be convinced that some of it is. I don't think they'd treat him the same way if he were a white dude named "Adam Tucker." .
Lastly, let me qualify something. I do certainly feel that people have cut Obama many less breaks as president than they would if he were white. LaTavia mentioned many of the major things that the man has done since becoming president and many of them were things that he said he'd do (even though some I personally don't like I gotta admit he did them and helped us avoid another great depression). I personally feel that Obama did more in his first 100 days than Bush did in 8 years.
September 5 at 6:11pm

Kevin quick clerical clarification, Bruce. They did impeach him, they just didn't convict him. Impeachment is just putting someone on trial. You still have to convict them to get them out.
September 5 at 6:14pm

--END THREAD --

Vann:
"I (still) pledge allegiance to the flag of the United States of America and to the republic for which it stands, one nation under God (YHWH) with liberty and justice for all."
September 10 at 3:40pm

Dana Nuheritage I don't. I see it as a violation of the 10 Commandments? And exactly what does the flag represent? I hope it represents the ppl here. And where do the ppl here come from? Answer: from all over the world. So what exactly is this thing we call America? Hopefully not the dirt. We shld b loyal to no patch of dirt. Hopefully not the buildings. There r buildings all around the world. Prior to Obama being elected, I wldn't even stand for the Anthem. It's all idolatry to me.
September 10 at 4:49pm

Vann which commandment?
September 10 at 5:55pm

Matthew Dana, that was the most ignorant thing I've ever read. Please do us all a favor and dont vote or procreate
September 10 at 5:16pm

Dana Nuheritage @ Vann: "U shall not make for urslf an idol." Matthew it's too late for ur admonishing. Butt just w8, u r young. U shall hear more that ur youthful ears will consider foolish. "A fool shows his annoyance at once."
September 10 at 5:24pm

Matthew So you're saying either you cant see a difference between a nation and a god or that you dont think others can? You do realize that God ordained nations and peoples? A pledge to a nation is not worship to a god and your...argument...that we shouldn't be loyal to our country simply because our ancestors came from another place is one of the most ridiculous things I've ever heard. Abraham came from a different place but he founded Israel, according to you the Israelis should not be loyal to the Promised Land and just hand

Jerusalem over to the muslims. It's just dirt and buildings and there's lots of those, right?
September 10 at 5:30pm

Matthew and speaking of Idolatry, what does obama being president have to do with whether you stand for the National Anthem or not?
September 10 at 5:31pm

Dana Nuheritage My thoughts can b no clearly expressed than in the form that I wrote them. If u disagree w/ my opinions, so be it. I bid u peace.
Ass for matters that u grafted on to what I wrote, where did I say a ppl shld not b loyal to their nation? U shld consult a dictionary to learn the definition of 'nation'. A nation is a group of ppl, not a geographical entity. The geographical entity is the 'nation state'. This country uprooted the Cherokee nation on the March of Tears. Were they less of a nation b/c this gov't placed them n concentration camps on another plot of dirt?
In regards to ur confusion of the issue by bringing up Isreal, don't confuse the present day Isreali w/ the Hebrews Moses led out of Egypt. Butt I know, ur indoctrination into what u believe u think the Bible says prevents u from understand this point. 'For truth is foolishness for those who r perishing'.
September 10 at 5:50pm

Matthew You've outdone yourself, THAT was the most ignorant thing I've ever read and it brings Prov 26:4 to mind. I'll just say that you should really work on your spelling, punctuation and grammar if you're going to be so bombastic, arrogant and condescending. Enjoy feeling right because I wont respond again.
September 10 at 6:10pm

Dana Nuheritage If butt Ize was ass ntelignt ass u bees massuh & wnt at dems finerest nstituteses of lurning just liken u had done; den Ize wld undrstnd moe duh wordz cumming out ur anuholes.
September 10 at 6:47pm

Stephanie Once again Bruce you have succeeded in getting people fired up!!! Lol...
September 10 at 8:11pm

– END THREAD –

Kira:
just interviewed Dick Cheney. No one got shot.
September 12 at 1:18pm

Sasan Ok I'm against shooting too, did you at least get a nice juicy slap in?
September 12 at 2:50pm

Steve that's too bad...(HIM, not YOU, or course!)
September 12 at 2:58pm

Steve Did u take a shower yet? Dont know if that slime comes off!
September 12 at 2:58pm

Dana Nuheritage I trust u asked tougher questions then the ones asked of him to date. A toughie like: Is this book of urs a self-serving attempt to exonerate ur name to future historians?
September 12 at 5:11pm

Kira So how do you all really feel Dana? That would be what we call a leading question, counselor.
September 12 at 5:15pm

Dana Nuheritage Technically not. A leading question is one that suggests the answer, eg. Didn't u write this book just to justify ur nvolvement w/ the Bush Adm universally condemned policies? Butt I wld agree it is not an open ended question.
September 12 at 5:20pm

Steve Sadly, it matters not what one asks. He will give the answer to the question he wants asked, and it will never be to admit that he f&*%ed us all, encouraged (and enjoyed) "enhanced interrogation techniques", and cost America trillions of dollars and thousands of lives (likely HUNDREDS of thousands lives if you count Iraqi's and Afghani's (which I am quite sure he does NOT!)
September 12 at 5:25pm

Zalan Wow... interesting point of view you have Steve, I wonder if you felt the same way about Clinton, who couldn't figure out the meaning of the word "is" - Rhodes scholar that he is and all... At least Cheney had enough guts to stand by what he believed in (not sure if anyone has ever made the point about him enjoying any kind of interrogation techniques, or that's just a typical tactic of the radicals on both sides - to vilify people that disagree with them).
September 12 at 9:18pm

Dana Nuheritage Steve's point of view is not that interesting or unique. Millions n America share that opinion and billions around the world do ass well . To disagree w/ it is one thing. Butt to suggest having it means he condones Clinton's actions or is proof of radical leanings, is to engage n the sort of disinformation practiced by the world's greatest despotic regimes. U, urslf, r actually guilty of the very thing u accuse Steve of: 'viligy[ing] ppl tht disagree w/ [u].'
September 12 at 9:38pm

Rochelle Well, keep in mind, as they say, "When Clinton lied, no one died." The two men's "indiscretions" are not even comparable.
September 12 at 9:39pm

– END THREAD –

Monica:
"Truth lies within ourselves; it takes no rise from outward things, whate'er you may believe. There is an inmost center in us all, where truth abides in fullness and to know rather consists in opening out a way whence the imprisoned splendor may escape than in effecting entry for light supposed to be without."-Robert Browning
September 16,2011 at 10:15am

> **Monica** i don't quite understand the last part of the final sentence, but i love this quote.
> September 16,2011 at 10:19am
>
> **Dana Nuheritage** If truth lies w/n us, don't lies reside w/n us ass well?
> September 16, 2011 at 10:33am
>
> **Monica** dana: i feel that this is more speaking to the truth/reality of our true Self, our true nature. Not so much as in "right or wrong" or "telling the truth or lies."
> September 16, 2011 at 11:43am
>
> **Dana Nuheritage** In that case, is not truth AND reality w/n us?
> September 16, 2011 at 11:50am
>
> **Monica** and it's our responsibility to uncover what is clouding our truth. and to discern which is which
> September 16, 2011 at 11:56am

Dana Nuheritage Butt isn't our reality our truth and our truth our reality? The person that believes she is n total control of her life is right. The person that believes he has no control of his life is also right. 'Nothing is good or bad xcpt our minds make it so'.
September 16, 2011 at 12:20pm

Monica dana are you purposefully writing "butt" and "ass?"
September 16, 2011 at 1:20pm

Dana Nuheritage Huhhhhhh?
September 16, 2011 at 1:28pm

Monica check your spelling and choice of words.
September 16, 2011 at 1:37pm

Colin someone's mind just may be in the gutter...
September 16, 2011 at 2:15pm

DENOUEMENT

Just prior to this book going to print some events were reported in the media that Radu felt compelled to comment on. They are added here without dates and times.

That reverend who said Mormonism is a cult and that's y the GOP shldn't nominate Romney, watching him tells me one thing: It tells me how Barney Fife wld look and gesture if he were a back-water, country preacher. Except Barney had a pure heart.

I thought Dave Chappelle's portrayal of the Black White-Supremacist was a fictional character 'til I started listening to Herman Cain running for Collaborator-in-Chief. The day they unveiled the King memorial in DC to the nation he further unveiled himself on Meet the Press to the GOP. If it were left to him, MLK wld have 'sat quietly in the back of the bus and stayed out of trouble.' R we sure he isn't the CEO of the Godfather Fried Chicken and Seedless Watermelons chain?

Was Kris Humphries even in the game long enough to get a shot off? Did he have time to take it to the house and jam his balls thru the hole before being ejected by Kim Kardashian? Did he at least consummate his selection after pledging allegiance on the court before being taken to court? Plz tell me he did cum to realize before being told to hit the showers, ass we all do, tht having a big, back court doesn't mean ur big man has license to dunk anytime he wants to.

> <u>Melanie</u> I just found out he is half Black
>
> <u>Dana Nuheritage</u> his attraction to that phat @$$ of hers wasn't a clue?
>
> Maybe that was the problem. The right half isn't Black. Marrying a man that tall she felt that she should be able to do chin-ups in the comfort of her own bedroom.

A 10th woman has come forward to accuse Herman Cain of sexual harassment. She was, until recently, a reporter covering the GOP presidential campaign. She said Cain told her his 9-9-9 Plan was inspired by the length of his manhood. In response Cain denied this latest accusation ass well. He said it was a simple misunderstanding. He said what he actually told her is that his 9-9-9 Plan was inspired by the height of his white hood.

MF reminds me of Show & Tell when I was in elementary school. Only a very few kids would present any thing of interest that enthralled the entire class. The vast majority of what was shared left me wondering how in the world does this student think anyone in this class is interested in knowing about that. If your classmates weren't interested in what your family had for dinner in elementary school, they are probably not interested now in seeing pictures of the meal you are about to eat or ate 48 hours ago.

This 'let's go see Redtails to send Hollywood a message movement' misses the whole point. Hollywood already knows that 'black movies' (whatever that means) are marketable. Look at the success of Glory, I am Legend, Sugar Hill, Precious, Training Day and a whole host of other movies. For whatever reason, they don't want to tell your stories. So a la Bollywood and Tyler Perry, no matter how you feel about those films, pool your capital and make your own movies. Leave Hollywood to Hollywood. Then maybe people of color in this world won't be brain washed to believe that their hair must be dyed blond to be considered attractive.

Tonight at the 2011 Grammys you may get treated to some 'Acceptance Speech Christianity.' That's when America awards artists who put out songs with misogynistic, violent and narcissistic themes they justify by claims of 'I'm getting paid.' Then they thank their lord and savior for their prizes. The closest parallel to this phenomenon is 'Founding Fathers' Faith': That's when you steal a land, enslave a people and commit genocide then dedicate your work to life, liberty and the pursuit of happiness for all mankind as commanded by god.

Watching clips of the Grammy performances confirms something I realized many moons ago. The more talented artists are the fewer people they need on stage with them. The really talented can stand before an audience with just their voice or instrument and lay themselves bare to entertain. Those with the least talent have so many people onstage with them you can hardly make them out. That is a Freudian effort to hide before an audience so that they are not found out and called out for their lack of talent.

Rick Santorum, a Catholic, says Obama follows a phony theology not based on the Bible. That's like Newt Gingrich preaching hold sacred the marital bed. Where in the Bible does Santorum see an army of celibate priests telling everyone else how to practice their faith? Has he not read Jesus' words, 'Call no man on earth father (pope is derived from a Greek word meaning father) for you have one father in heaven?' Where in the Bible does he see Jesus seeking election to the Sanhedrin? I could go on and point out such inconsistencies in any religion but how uninformed do you have to be about your own faith to give credence to such dribble?

A lone 17 year old black kid in a white hoody enjoying the fruit of his purchase is considered a threat to life and limb by this Republic. A gang of whites wearing white hoods destroying life & limb to sow strange fruit are considered heroes of the Republic for the Birth of a Nation. America: Home of the Free and Land of the Scared.

Our criminal justice system is the envy of the Free World. Here, law enforcement will duly deliberate ad infinitum to insure that would be defendants are not even arrested in the absence of sufficient evidence to remotely implicate them in a crime. If Bin Laden had been arrested in Sanford, FL prior to meeting Seal Team 6, police there would have questioned him about his involvement in 911, released him after 15 minutes and told him they'll be in touch--maybe. After all, who really knows what happened on those planes. The passengers are dead and in the videos he released about his involvement, he never shows a receipt for a ticket on any of the flights. As for those death row inmates released because of incontrovertible DNA evidence, well...they were wearing hoodies at the time of their arrest.

Watching Witney Houston's Memorial Service (When I was young they called those things funerals. I guess the promoters of that show didn't want to scare potential viewers away with references that could possibly evoke thoughts of our mortality.) reminded me of my travels through Western Europe. Every time I've been there I happened to see some kind of advertisement, usually a poster or flyer, for an African American gospel choir there touring. I think this nation takes for granted how powerful that music is and doesn't know how appreciated is the music of the Black church around the world. It had to be powerful to comfort a people through slavery, lynchings, Jim Crow and persecution.

-END BOOK 1 of 3 -